Pub Walks in
SOUTH-WEST CORNWALL

Tricia and David Rowe

COUNTRYSIDE BOOKS
NEWBURY BERKSHIRE

COUNTRYSIDE BOOKS
3 Catherine Road
Newbury, Berkshire

To view our complete range of books,
please visit us at
www.countrysidebooks.co.uk

ISBN 1 85306 682 6

To our family, with love

Photographs by the authors
Maps by the authors and redrawn by Gelder design & mapping
Designed by Graham Whiteman

Typeset by Techniset Typesetters, Newton-le-Willows
Produced through MRM Associates Ltd., Reading
Printed by Woolnough Bookbinding Ltd., Irthlingborough

Contents

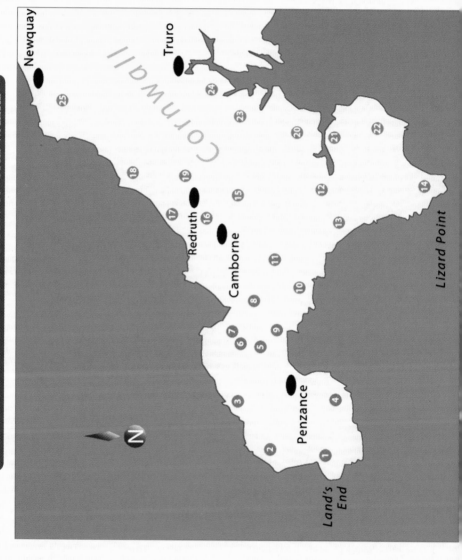

PUBLISHER'S NOTE

We hope that you obtain considerable enjoyment from this book; great care has been taken in its preparation. However, changes of landlord and actual closures are sadly not uncommon. Likewise, although at the time of publication all routes followed public rights of way or permitted paths, diversion orders can be made and permissions withdrawn.

We cannot, of course, be held responsible for such diversion orders and any inaccuracies in the text which result from these or any other changes to the routes nor any damage which might result from walkers trespassing on private property. We are anxious though that all details covering the walks and the pubs are kept up to date and would therefore welcome information from readers which would be relevant to future editions.

The sketch maps accompanying each walk are not always to scale and are intended to guide you to the starting point and give a simple but accurate idea of the route to be taken. For those who like the benefit of detailed maps, we recommend that you arm yourself with the relevant Ordnance Survey map in the Explorer series.

Walking Cornwall comes highly recommended; we love it! In our opinion there is nowhere like it, so varied, so special. Atmosphere abounds in Cornwall. Everything is so neatly contained within our natural boundaries for we are nearly an island. We are bordered on all sides by water with the exception of a few miles before the River Tamar starts its journey to the sea. It is easy to get away from it all in Cornwall, as our walks will show. The landscape changes so quickly here, from wild moorland to gentle farmland, to panoramic seascapes, rugged cliffs and wonderful beaches, to the stark beauty of our mining heritage and the mysteries of our standing stones. Our walks in South-West Cornwall, which encompasses the area south-west of a line from Newquay to Truro and as far as Land's End, cover all these variations, to give an overall view of our part of the world.

Walkers always have somewhere to go and we are no exception. We have walked the Cornwall Coastal Footpath from Marsland Mouth in the north to Cremyll on Plymouth Sound in the south, not all at once, but in day-sized chunks. There is camaraderie amongst walkers. There is always a greeting and, more often than not, a chat about where they have come from and where they are going. Life in Cornwall is led at a more leisurely pace and a word often used is 'dreckly' the equivalent of Spain's 'mañana'.

Each walk starts and ends at a good pub which caters for the walker's needs whether it is a bar snack or a full meal, giving the chance to sample Cornish ales and the pub's culinary specialities. Telephone numbers are provided should you wish to make enquiries. Low beamed ceilings are a feature of many of our Cornish pubs, setting the mood of the place and giving it a sense of history. Several are linked to tin mining and smuggling and at least three have a ghost. Our sincere thanks to the landlords of the pubs we have visited for the warm welcome we have received from all of them. Parking is usually available for pub patrons, but please do seek permission before leaving your car while you are away on your walk. If there is a public car park nearby it is always preferable to use it – and if you do park elsewhere, please be careful not to block any farm gateways or tracks.

Care must be taken on the coastal footpath, keeping to the path, also in the mining areas and children should be stringently supervised at all times. Most of the routes are suitable for the average walker and family groups with the exception of Walks 1, 2, 3 and 4 which are more strenuous and are designed for the more seasoned walker. The average length of the walks is 5 miles, making an ideal half-day ramble and leaving ample time to visit the attractions detailed. The walks range from 2 to 8 miles, with several circuits having distance variations, which can be adapted to suit the needs of the walker. We recommend walking boots or at least strong shoes. Be prepared for any weather and carry a waterproof. Water and a light snack are a good idea especially if the energy starts to fade. When crossing farmland please respect the farmer's crops and livestock, shut all gates and take your rubbish home and keep dogs under control at all times.

Above all enjoy these walks. We may pass you somewhere along the way!

Tricia and David Rowe

Sennen Churchtown
The First and Last Inn

MAP: OS EXPLORER 102 (GR 357255)	**WALK 1**	**DISTANCE:** 4 OR 6 MILES

DIRECTIONS TO START: SENNEN VILLAGE IS SITUATED ON THE A30 WEST OF PENZANCE, ABOUT A MILE FROM LAND'S END. **PARKING:** THERE IS A CAR PARK FOR PATRONS AT THE PUB, BUT PLEASE ASK PERMISSION BEFORE YOU LEAVE YOUR CAR WHILE YOU WALK.

The walk starts in Sennen Churchtown, high above the coast, and taking footpaths wends its way down to the sweep of golden sand at Sennen Cove, far below, with wonderful views across Whitesand Bay to Cape Cornwall. We arrive at the coast amid the soft white sand dunes of Sunny Corner and follow the coastal path to the fishing village of Sennen Cove.

The walk to Land's End passes Maen Cliff lookout and Maen Cliff Castle. There are several strange shaped and strangely named rocks around Land's End including the Armed Knight, the Irish Lady, the arched Enys Dodnan, Dr Syntax's Head and Dr Johnson's Head. Add to that the unusual pillared rock formations of Land's End and it makes for a very dramatic walk, with views of the Longships lighthouse offshore. At Nanjizal Bay we turn inland and head back across the fields to the First and Last Inn.

The First and Last Inn

The pub sign reads 'First Inn in England' on one side and 'Last Inn in England' on the other. A pub with two names? Well that is not its only claim to fame. At the end of the bar is a deep, glass-topped well. The inscription reads: 'Annie's well c1620'. Annie, a former landlady, used this entrance to a smugglers' tunnel running to the cliffs, to indulge in smuggling and wrecking. After turning Queen's evidence against one of her smuggling associates she was staked out on Sennen beach and drowned by the incoming tide. It is said that the small buildings behind the inn were used to stable the donkeys used by the wreckers.

The inn has a large bar with an adjoining non-smoking dining room, and a beer garden. Children are welcome, as are dogs on the lead. There is a good selection of lunchtime food including a choice of vegetarian dishes and a very popular Sunday roast, and in the evening speciality menus for theme nights. Beers on offer are Hicks local ale and guest ales from Bass and Tetley.

Opening times in the summer are 11 am to 11 pm on Monday to Saturday and 12 noon to 10.30 pm on Sundays. Winter opening times are 11 am to 3 pm and 5.30 pm to 11 pm with all day opening at weekends (11 am to 11 pm on Saturdays and 12 noon to 10.30 pm on Sundays). Food is served from 12 noon to 2 pm and 6 pm to 9 pm. Telephone: 01736 871680.

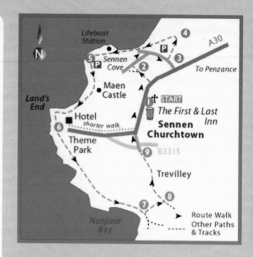

The Walk

① Leave the pub and turn right, heading along the pavement beside the main road. Take the footpath on the left just before Sennen Post Office. After the second stile, follow the arrow straight ahead, and head for a wooden stile in the opposite hedge and into Maria's Lane.

② Turn right, and at the main road, cross and turn right again heading uphill, passing a car park.

③ Take the footpath on the left leading to Sunny Corner. Follow this path, crossing two small bridges. About 10 yards after the second bridge turn left down a path, heading for cottages below.

④ When you reach these, turn left and take the path between the last two cottages. You now join the coastal path, which leads into Sennen Cove. It was here, in 1497, that Perkin Warbeck landed, in an unsuccessful attempt to claim the throne of England. The official coastal path leads through the village,

The Round House and harbour, Sennen Cove

winding around the Round House, now an art gallery and craft shop, which originally housed the capstan used to pull boats up the slipway above which it stands. Walk through the village picking up the coastal path after passing the lifeboat station.

⑤ Go through the car park and follow the coastal footpath up steps, passing Maen Cliff lookout and Maen Cliff Castle. Just below the lookout is a rock called the Irish Lady, said to be named after a lady who initially survived a shipwreck there, but subsequently perished on the rock itself. Continue to Land's End, passing the First & Last House.

⑥ At this point the walk can be shortened by leaving the Land's End complex by the main entrance and following the pavement for about a mile to the pub.

Otherwise continue, passing the Land's End Hotel and bearing right for the coastal footpath again, down steps, over a bridge and taking the steps ahead. Follow the path beside Greeb Small Animal Farm and Craft Centre, which is on the left. Continue on the coastal footpath until just before Nanjizal Bay

PLACES OF INTEREST NEARBY

Museum of Submarine Telegraphy in Porthcurno, reached to the south off the B3315. This wartime communications centre is housed in a series of tunnels set in the cliffs and includes a unique collection of historical equipment which dates back to the 1870s. Open 10 am to 5 pm on Sunday to Friday from April to June and September to October and every day from July to August, also Bank Holiday Saturdays. For winter opening times telephone: 01736 810966.

The Irish Lady

¼ mile, high above the valley. Ignore a path to the right and shortly afterwards go through a kissing gate.

⑧ Go straight ahead across a field. Sennen church can be seen in the distance over the fields. Cross the next field keeping the hedge on your right. Straight across the third field and then continue with the hedge on your left and go out of a gate into a lane, passing cottages at Trevilley. When the lane meets a road, cross and go over a stile and through a farmyard. Leave the farmyard by a stile and continue with the hedge on your right, passing a Cornish Cross on the other side of the hedge. Cross another stile and follow the path, with the hedge on your left, to a kissing gate. Immediately after this cross another stile and emerge onto the gravel driveway of a cottage. The path passes the cottage and continues out of the gate onto the road.

where an arrowed post beside some standing stones directs you to the left.

⑦ Leaving the coastal footpath we climb steeply inland. Follow this path for about

⑨ Take the road opposite and when you reach the main road, turn right and head along the pavement to the First and Last Inn in England.

St Just
The Star Inn

MAP: OS EXPLORER 102 (GR 371313)

WALK 2

DISTANCE: 5 MILES

DIRECTIONS TO START: ST JUST IS REACHED ON THE A3071 WHICH JOINS THE A30 JUST SOUTH-WEST OF PENZANCE. **PARKING:** IN THE MAIN FREE CAR PARK IN THE CENTRE OF ST JUST.

St Just is a small, busy town about 6 miles from Land's End. It was once the centre of an active mining industry and although the mines have now gone the town still retains the feeling of a lively community. The walk takes us through fields, over stiles and down the remote Kenidjack Valley where the relics of tin mining stand quietly covered in ivy. In its heyday this area would have been buzzing with mining activity and the centre of a very close knit community. We accompany the busy little river down the valley and join the coastal path to follow it westwards to Cape Cornwall, which has the distinction of being the only cape in England. From Carn Gloose we have views ahead of Sennen and Land's End, and on the horizon, on a clear day, the Isles of Scilly are visible. One feels one could almost reach out and touch them.

We then follow the coastal footpath through Cot Valley to Porth Nanven. At Gribba Head, with views of the Longships lighthouse, Sennen and Land's End ahead, we turn inland and head back to St Just following the paths and lanes of West Penwith.

The Star Inn

The Star Inn, in the centre of St Just, is a real find. Squeezed in amongst the buildings of the main street it has hanging baskets outside (in season!) and a notice on the door proclaiming it a stress free zone. The building, as it is now, dates from 1740, but there was a pub on this site previously. Its low-beamed bar is decorated with hanging tankards and the walls are hung with mining samples and old mining photographs, which overflow onto the ceiling as they ran out of walls! This is the sort of pub to linger in, a place where time has stood still.

The Star Inn has two celebrity regulars who are to be seen propping up the bar on their favourite stools every evening. Their names are Georgie, the pub dog, and his friend Benji who lives down the road. There is the one bar, a separate room for children and a beer garden. Beers on offer are Cornish, Daylight Robbery and Hicks, and Tinners straight from the barrel. The pub also does very good food, specialising in fresh local crab and home-made dishes.

Opening times on Monday to Saturday in the summer are 11 am to 11 pm. In winter (October-Easter) 11 am to 11 pm, but closed from 3 pm to 6 pm on Tuesdays, Wednesdays and Thursdays. Sundays all year: 12 noon to 10.30 pm. Food is served from 12 noon to 2 pm and 6.30 pm to 8.30 pm all through the year. Accommodation is available in the form of three double bedrooms. Telephone: 01736 788767.

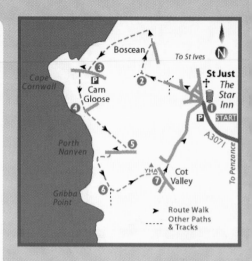

Route Walk
Other Paths & Tracks

The Walk

① Leave the Star Inn and turn right, heading for the main square. At the clock tower cross the road and continue into Boswedden Road. Go straight ahead at the crossroads, passing the school on your left. Where the road veers right, carry straight on, passing two cottages and following a grassy lane. At the end of the lane cross over a stile, following the path across the field. Cross another stile beside a gateway and continue with the hedge on your left. About 30 yards before a gate there is a stile on your left.

② Ignore this but immediately turn right, following the path over several fields and stiles to Boscean, where the path runs along the top of the hedge and into a lane by the farm buildings. Turn left and continue down the lane with mines on your right. At the bottom of this lane cross the river and turn sharp left. At the National Trust sign for Kenidjack bear left down the valley. At the big house take the path on the left marked 'coastal path'. Cross the bridge over the river and follow

Kenidjack Valley

the coastal path signs. Continue to the road at Cape Cornwall.

③ Turn right and then left at the bottom of the hill, again following the coastal footpath. A steep climb brings you to Carn Gloose viewpoint.

④ Bear right and continue along the coast path and down into Cot Valley. Care must be taken to keep to the path, as there are numerous mineshafts in this area.

⑤ At the road turn sharp right and continue to a picnic site. Treacherous rocks called The Brisons overlook the bay here, and they have claimed many a ship. Between 1971 and 1992 local man Willie Oates and his friend Jack Angwin spent much of their time making seats in the rock, cobbling paths and tending the

coastal walkway, which all stands as a lasting memory of their love of this stretch of the coast. Relax on one of their seats, take in the view and let the world pass you by – and spare a thought for the diligence of these men and the sheer effort it must have taken to get materials so far along these paths. Take the path to the left,

PLACES OF INTEREST NEARBY

Geevor Tin Mine at Pendeen, north of St Just, ceased working in 1990 but now gives to the public an overall view of Cornwall's industrial past. This all weather visitor centre includes surface and underground tours together with a museum and café. Open on Monday to Friday, 10 am to 4 pm, from January to March and November to mid December; Sunday to Friday and Bank Holiday Saturdays, 10 am to 5 pm, from April to October. Telephone: 01736 788662.

Cape Cornwall and The Brisons

over the river, and join the coastal path again. Continue along the coastal footpath for about a mile and when you reach a stile, ignore it.

⑥ At this point turn left, leaving the coast and heading inland along a grassy path. Cross a stile at the end of this path going straight over a field and onto a track, turning left. Enter a field and keep the hedge on your left. Leave this field following the yellow arrowed marker post, bearing right and into another field and heading for the gateway diagonally opposite. At the gateway follow the yellow arrow to the left keeping the hedge on your left. Leave this field over a stile by a gate, passing cottages. Continue straight ahead.

⑦ At the T-junction by the Youth Hostel sign, turn right and almost immediately turn left over a stile, following the footpath sign at Lower Cot Mill. After 100 yards the path enters a field. Continue with the hedge on your left, and go over a further two stiles and into a lane. Walk straight ahead and at a junction keep left and continue into St Just.

Treen
The Gurnard's Head Hotel

MAP: OS EXPLORER 102 (GR 436376)	WALK 3	DISTANCE: 2½ OR 6 MILES

DIRECTIONS TO START: TREEN IS ON THE COAST ROAD, THE B3306, BETWEEN ST JUST AND ST IVES. YOU WILL FIND THE GURNARD'S HEAD HOTEL JUST WEST OF ZENNOR. **PARKING:** IN THE HOTEL'S CAR PARK, BUT PLEASE ASK PERMISSION IF LEAVING YOUR CAR WHILE YOU WALK.

Parts of this walk are fairly strenuous, not so much for the rise and fall of the path, but for its uneven nature. If you want to look at the view, stop first! We join the coastal path above Treen Cove, passing the ruined engine house, where cliffside greenery reaches almost to the sea in places, and where pilchard fishing and packing once flourished. The aroma of clifftop foliage followed us as we walked this wild stretch of coast, passing Gurnard's Head, which does indeed resemble the head of the fish of that name. Great granite boulders are scattered over the moorland landscape, giving it a dramatic and isolated look, although the main coast road isn't too far away.

At Porthmeor Cove we turn inland and pass through Bosigran Farm, via the church path, before circling the slopes of Carn Galver, an imposing rocky ridge that stands at 816 feet. This is a steady ½ mile ascent and it is not until you look back that you realise how far you have climbed, and take time to admire the views. As you round Carn Galver there are views diagonally to the right of Hannibal's Carn with the Gurnard's Head Hotel in the distance, and in the middle distance fine examples of ancient field systems. Leaving the slopes of Carn Galver we rejoin the road and then follow the church path to the east for a short distance before returning to the Gurnard's Head Hotel.

The Gurnard's Head Hotel

This 17th century coaching inn describes itself as a traditional Cornish country pub with good food and comfortable accommodation. Situated a stone's throw from the coastal footpath, it boasts panoramic coastal and moorland views. There are two large bars and an extensive garden seating area. The main bar is decorated with a large collection of paintings, some of nearby Gurnard's Head.

Beers on offer are Cornish Knocker, London Pride and Flowers Original, and there is a full range of wines. There are separate lunch and evening menus, with specials boards, the speciality of the house being seafood. Emphasis is on fresh local produce and ingredients. Children and dogs are welcome, but no children in the main bar. Accommodation is available in the form of en suite rooms all with either coastal or moorland views.

Opening times are 12 noon to 3 pm and 6 pm to 11 pm; Sundays 12 noon to 4 pm and 7 pm to 10.30 pm; open all day from 12 noon in August. Food is served from 12 noon to 2.30 pm and 6.30 pm to 9.15 pm. Live music is a regular weekly feature here, drawing on the talents of local musicians and a variety of instruments. Telephone: 01736 796928.

The Walk

① Leave the hotel and turn left and down the single-track lane beside it. After about 100 yards you pass through the hamlet of Treen, after which the lane develops into

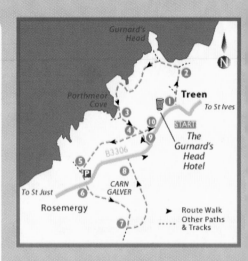

a track heading towards the coast. The track meanders down towards the sea for about ½ mile, passing a derelict mine building. Some 200 yards after this the coastal path crosses it.

② Turn left and follow this. Just before Gurnard's Head the path splits; take the left-hand fork and continue following the coastal footpath, with views ahead of the lighthouse at Pendeen Watch. At Porthmeor Cove, a lonely, boulder-

PLACES OF INTEREST NEARBY

Wayside Folk Museum, at Zennor (just a short distance along the road towards St Ives) houses a collection of over 5,000 items in 16 display areas, including the cobbler's shop, wheelwright's, laundry and mill, plus an extensive collection of photographs and information on people who have lived in the area. The visitor can handle many of the exhibits. Open on Sunday to Friday, also Saturdays during school holidays and bank holiday weekends, 11 am to 5 pm in April and October and 10 am to 6 pm from May to the end of September. Last entry to museum 45 minutes before closing. Telephone: 01736 796945.

Gurnard's Head

strewn bay, you cross a mini clapper bridge over a stream, going up the steps and over a low stile.

③ Continue following the coastal path for about 50 yards, then turn left following the path inland. Cross a stile beside a gate and continue uphill, passing the buildings of the grist mill and the tin stamps which were used to crush the rock in the initial stages of tin processing.

④ Where the paths cross, turn right following the church path. (If you want to shorten the walk here, turn left to return to the pub, following the instructions from point 9.) The path eventually heads across a field and over a stile to Bosigran Farm. Cross the farmyard, turning right and following the yellow arrowed path ahead, through two consecutive wooden gates beside a wooden barn. Cross four fields over stiles, leaving the fourth field by a stile in the left-hand hedge. Cross field five diagonally, leaving by a stile, making a total of five stiles. Cross fields six and seven via gates, emerging onto rough boulder-strewn ground. Continue straight ahead, veering slightly to the right and going through a gap in a stone hedge into the next field. Cross this, bearing right and exiting through a gap on the right between two wooden gateposts. Cross diagonally, taking the left-hand gap in a stone wall. Continue straight ahead. After 200 yards you join up with the path that leads from the coast up to the Carn Galver mine buildings.

⑤ Turn left and head towards the mine engine houses. Cross a stile beside a metal gate and take the right-hand path leading to the road.

Carn Galver mine buildings

⑥ At the road, turn right and after 50 yards, turn left following a public footpath sign. We are now taking to the moorland area of the slopes of Carn Galver which is the dramatic rocky ridge to your left. Follow the track steadily uphill for about ½ mile and when the path forks towards Carn Galver summit, ignore this and continue straight ahead.

⑦ After a further ½ mile, take the path to the left, between two hedges, to round Carn Galver summit. Follow the track down the other side of the carn, with sea views ahead, and enter the road opposite Bosigran Farm.

⑧ Turn right and continue for about 400 yards before taking a grassy footpath on the left. Cross a stile beside a gate and continue along the path. Where paths cross, ignore the coastal footpath sign and turn right.

⑨ Follow the church path over a stile into a field. Go straight across this field and over two consecutive stiles into a lane by cottages.

⑩ Turn right to the road. Turn left and follow the road, with care, for about ¼ mile back to the Gurnard's Head Hotel.

Lamorna
The Lamorna Wink

| MAP: OS EXPLORER 102 (GR 446246) | **WALK 4** | DISTANCE: 5½ MILES |

DIRECTIONS TO START: TURN OFF THE B3315 SOUTH-WEST OF NEWLYN, FOLLOWING SIGNS FOR LAMORNA. **PARKING:** IN THE WINTER YOU CAN LEAVE YOUR CAR IN THE LAMORNA WINK CAR PARK WHILE YOU WALK, BUT PLEASE ASK PERMISSION FIRST. IN SUMMER USE THE PAY CAR PARK IN LAMORNA COVE, JUST DOWN THE HILL.

If you are interested in stones The Merry Maidens at the beginning of this walk will be of interest to you. A short distance further along we pass Tregiffian Burial Chamber, which was built between 3000 BC and 2000 BC. Shortly after this we turn towards the coast and follow woodland paths down to the unique setting of St Loy's Cove where a mass of symmetrically rounded boulders litter the foreshore piled one upon the other and not a space between them.

Further along this stretch of coastline are the Tater Du lighthouse and the former cottage home of Derek and Jean Tangye where the well-loved *Minack Chronicles* were written. Entering Lamorna Cove, around the headland you are greeted with the stark beauty of the granite spoils of long ago quarrying. Stone from here was used in the building of the Thames Embankment. The Lamorna Valley is well known for its artists' colony in the early 1900s.

The Lamorna Wink

Situated halfway down the steep Lamorna Valley, this pub gets its name from the Kiddleywink licences of 1830, when for 2 guineas and a surety of £20 it was possible to obtain a licence to sell beer six days a week. In the days of smuggled liquor it is said that a wink to the landlord would produce something much stronger than beer and the inn sign illustrates this. The Winds was originally two cottages and the artist Sir Alfred Munnings lived here in the early 20th century.

The Wink has one bar and a dining area and plenty of outside seating. Children and dogs are welcome. Beers on offer are the Cornish draughts of Sharp's Doom Bar and Skinner's. There is a good choice of bar food, the emphasis being on fresh ingredients and the speciality being fresh crab salad.

Opening times are 11 am to 4 pm and 6 pm to 11 pm, Sundays 12 noon to 4 pm and 6 pm to 10.30 pm. Food is served at lunchtime from 11 am to 2.30 pm. Telephone: 01736 731566.

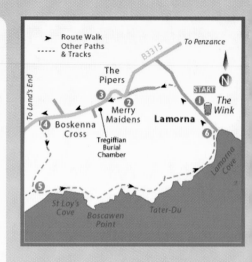

stile in the opposite hedge. As you cross this field, a glance to the right will give you a brief view of the Pipers standing stones. Once over the stile follow the path through the middle of the Merry Maidens to the road. These nineteen standing stones are said to date from the late Stone Age or Early Bronze Age. Legend has it that nineteen maidens danced on a Sunday and were unfortunate enough to be caught. The two musicians (the Pipers) who were with them weren't very lucky either; they are standing in the neighbouring field.

The Walk

① Leave the pub and turn right. After 300 yards take the public bridleway signposted to the left and climb steadily up this rocky path under trees. When you reach a road continue straight ahead passing Menwinnion Country House.

② On reaching the main road, immediately take the footpath to your left and follow a path across the field to a

PLACES OF INTEREST NEARBY

The Minack Theatre is carved into the cliffs above Porthcurno and it is here that a summer season of plays and musicals are performed to a backdrop of the sea. The Exhibition Centre tells the story of Rowena Cade who built this dramatic open air theatre with her own hands and made it her life's work. Open daily: 9.30 am to 5.30 pm from April to September and 10 am to 4 pm from October to March (closed from noon to 4.30 pm when there is a matinee). Telephone: 01736 810181.

The Merry Maidens Stone Circle

③ Turn left, a little further on passing Tregiffian Burial Chamber and Boskenna Cross and continue along this road for about ½ mile until you come to a sign for Boskenna Home Farm.

④ Turn left and follow the lane, which winds down through the farm buildings and houses. Where the lane bends to the right, continue along this signposted lane, passing more houses. Continue on this lane until it bears left, and at this point go straight ahead, through a metal gate, following a public footpath sign, continuing down a tarmac path. After 50 yards turn right into the woods where there is an arrow on a stone, immediately turning left down the valley following the arrow sign for the coastal footpath, with the stream on your right. Cross the stream on large boulders and turn left at the yellow arrow. Continue to a stile where you join the coastal footpath.

⑤ Cross this stile and immediately cross another stile on your left, heading down the valley, through rich vegetation and following the bubbling, energetic stream to the bouldered shores of St Loy's Cove. Cross over the boulders on the beach head and regain the coastal path, climbing steadily to Boscawen Point. From here you can see Tater Du lighthouse. The path now becomes more of an undulating path and easy walking which belies what it has in store, for the last stretch into Lamorna is quite strenuous, not because of the ups and downs but because of the boulder-strewn path.

⑥ Enter Lamorna and round the quayside, climbing the hill out of the cove and returning to the Lamorna Wink.

Ludgvan
The White Hart

MAP: OS EXPLORER 102 (GR 506331)	**WALK 5**	**DISTANCE:** 6½ MILES

DIRECTIONS TO START: TURN OFF THE HAYLE TO PENZANCE (A30) ROAD AT CROWLAS ONTO THE B3309. **PARKING:** LIMITED PARKING FOR PATRONS AT THE WHITE HART, BUT PLEASE ASK PERMISSION BEFORE LEAVING YOUR CAR WHILE YOU WALK. SOME ROADSIDE PARKING.

As with most walks in Cornwall there is a variety of scenery on this one. We leave the pub and follow paths and lanes parallel to the coast with marvellous views of Mount's Bay and St Michael's Mount, views that follow us for most of the route. Part of the walk follows the paths of the St Michael's Way, an ancient pilgrim route that starts at Lelant on the north coast and crosses the peninsula to St Michael's Mount on the south. Just before Gulval we cut down to the coast at Long Rock, crossing a footbridge over the main A30 and then the main railway line by a level crossing. From here we walk along the sea wall, beside the expanse of water dominated by St Michael's Mount, turning inland by Marazion Marsh to take to our country lanes again to return to Ludgvan.

The White Hart

This was built around the 14th century, originally as a church house to accommodate the masons who were brought in to build the church, which stands next door. It is known to have been an inn since the 1600s and is an inviting, dimly lit, traditional Cornish pub. There is one bar with low beams and panelled walls hung with old photographs and a few brasses and part of the bar itself is built on large barrels. Several snug eating areas are to be found to the left of the main door. There is also a delightful seating area in the garden at the rear and outside tables at the front. Children are welcome, but not in the bar area, and dogs are allowed in the pub.

A good selection of cask ales is available including Bass, Marston's and Flowers, and a range of wines. The menu offers a wide choice of dishes, supplemented each day by a variety of specials.

Opening times are 11 am to 2.30 pm and 6 pm to 11 pm; Sundays 12 noon to 3 pm and 7 pm to 10.30 pm. Food is served from 12 noon to 2 pm and 7 pm to 9 pm. Telephone: 01736 740574.

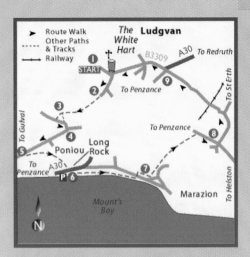

The Walk

① Leave the pub, turning right. At the church turn left, passing the information board for the St Michael's Way. Continue along this road until it bears left.

② At this point go straight ahead on a lane between houses, following an arrow marker, through a gate and straight ahead, picking up a narrow path, also arrowed. At the end of this path cross a stile into a lane and take the stile opposite into a field. Head directly across the field to the stile in the far fence, all marked with yellow arrows, and continue along the next field with the hedge on your right. On leaving this field, carry on straight ahead along the track, following the arrows. Where the track bears right into a field, ignore this and continue ahead, parallel with the coast. At a field continue with the hedge on your left. Three-quarters of the way down this field, the path takes to the hedge. Follow this into trees and over a bridge, followed by stepping-stones over a stream and into a lane.

③ Cross the lane into a field and head for a stile in the opposite hedge about 50 yards to the right of the gate. At the lane turn left. Continue straight ahead.

④ At a T-junction turn right. After the signpost for Poniou Farmhouse, ignore the first path on the right and follow the signposted path to Gulval, in the hedge,

Ludgvan

just after it, which runs along parallel to the road for two fields.

⑤ Leave the second field, enter the road and turn left, and after 20 yards take the footpath signposted on your right. Keep the hedge on your right and walk two sides of this field, leaving by a stile onto a narrow path in the far corner. You soon enter another field, and keeping the hedge on your left exit on a path through trees. At a lane turn right and cross the bridge over the A30. Pause for a moment, if you will, and take in the rush of modern day living down below! At the other end of the bridge continue straight on with St Michael's Mount in view ahead. When you meet the road at Long Rock, cross and take the road opposite leading to Long Rock beach across a level crossing.

⑥ At the coast turn left and follow the sea wall towards Marazion. After passing the Station Restaurant on the left, cross the car park and continue towards Marazion using the pavement opposite. If you have time, a visit to the RSPB nature reserve here at Marazion Marsh is well worthwhile. Over 230 species of bird have been recorded here, 480 species of insect and nearly 500 species of plant. In early winter starlings, sometimes in their

PLACES OF INTEREST NEARBY

Chysauster Ancient Village, $2\frac{1}{2}$ miles north-west of Gulval, is a prehistoric village dating from the late Iron Age. Consisting of eight well-preserved houses around a courtyard, it is said to be one of the best sites of its kind in the British Isles. Open daily from April to October, 10 am to 6 pm (5 pm in October). Telephone: 0831 757934.

Marazion Marsh

millions, arrive to stay in the reeds overnight. We have been there on several occasions when this vast cloud of birds has settled as we watched.

⑦ After about 400 yards turn left at a car park sign and cross the bridge, turning left and entering Green Lane. After 300 yards, soon after a sharp right bend, turn left down Green Lane West following a sign: 'Cart Track to Gwallon'. Walk along this road for about ½ mile and turn left before farm buildings between wooden posts, following the cycle track. Carry on along the tarmac track, which soon runs beside the Marazion bypass, until dropping down beside a bridge.

⑧ Turn left and go under the bridge and we rejoin the country lanes again. Continue along this road for about 1½ miles, ignoring the signpost for St Erth, following the sign for Crowlas and passing Truthwall Mill. The high hedges of Green Lane West are a mass of abundant foliage in June, harbouring pink campion, foxglove and honeysuckle, to name but a few. Certainly a Green Lane that lives up to its name! The church tower at Ludgvan is in our view in the distance for a good part of this lane.

⑨ At the crossroads take the road opposite, signposted to Ludgvan. Stay on this road now as it winds up the hill to the White Hart.

Cripplesease
The Engine Inn

| MAP: OS EXPLORER 102 (GR 500369) | **WALK 6** | DISTANCE: 6½ MILES |

DIRECTIONS TO START: CRIPPLESEASE IS SITUATED ON THE B3311 BETWEEN PENZANCE AND ST IVES. **PARKING:** THERE IS A CAR PARK FOR PATRONS AT THE ENGINE INN, BUT PLEASE ASK PERMISSION BEFORE LEAVING YOUR CAR WHILE YOU WALK.

A cuckoo followed us on this walk from start to finish. Whether it was the same cuckoo, we don't know, but we like to think it was! This circuit is particularly varied, passing through a diversity of well-marked paths, tracks and lanes, over farmland, where one field has a rustic seat in the corner, over moorland and downs, with panoramic views for miles around, and includes a variety of stiles. For most of the route we can look across and see the engine house near the Engine Inn. At one point there is a distant view of St Michael's Mount and Mount's Bay, and at another a glimpse of Godrevey lighthouse in St Ives Bay. On Lady Downs note the old style stone hedges, built stone upon stone, giving the landscape a wild and rugged look. We encountered a great number of rabbits on this walk and they scattered in all directions, as soon as they became aware of the vibration of our boots on the path. Just after the cottages at Skillywadden, we pass close by Towednack church, which was used in the filming of television's *Poldark* series.

The Engine Inn

The Engine Inn was built in 1680 and stands on high ground with panoramic views of the surrounding countryside. It has always been a pub and was named after the mine engine house of nearby Giew Mine, which closed in 1923, and doubled as the count house for the mine. Wages were paid through the window beside the main door and on pay-days the landlord provided free tow-rag – dry, salted white fish – in the hope that the miners would spend all their pay quenching their thirst afterwards! The atmosphere of the mining era is recreated with advertisement boards above the bar. There is a non-smoking dining room and outside patio area.

Beers on offer are Marston's Pedigree and Bass cask ales, together with a large range of keg ales, and there is a good selection of wines. There are extensive menu boards, the speciality being various steaks. Emphasis is on fresh local produce and meat, and home-cooked food. The Engine is very popular for Sunday lunches, when booking is essential.

Monday to Saturday opening times in summer are 11 am to 3 pm and 6 pm to 11 pm; in winter 12 noon to 2.30 pm and 7 pm to 11 pm. On Sundays the pub opens from 12 noon to 3 pm and 7 pm to 10.30 pm throughout the year. Food is served from 12 noon to 2 pm and 6 pm to 9 pm. En suite accommodation is available. Telephone: 01736 740204.

The Walk

① Leave the inn and turn right.

② After 200 yards follow the public footpath sign to the left by the Cripplesease sign. Pass a farm where the track turns into a grassy footpath through gorse. Go through a gate and there is a meeting of paths and a signpost with a multitude of arrows on it. Carry straight on. At the end of the path cross a stile and follow the public footpath sign to the left, keeping the hedge on your left.

③ Leave the field by a gate into a lane and turn right. At a crossroads turn right and continue along this road to a T-junction.

④ Turn right and continue along the lane to the village of Nancledra. At the main road, cross with care, turning right, and take the road almost immediately on the left, following the sign for Georgia, Embla and Amalveor. Follow this road for about ¼ mile until it forks. Turn left, following a further sign to Georgia, Embla and Amalveor.

Giew Mine Engine House

⑤ Proceed along this road for 200 yards, then take the track on your left, crossing a stream and climbing steadily uphill. When the tracks cross turn right and continue, passing Georgia Farm on your left and emerging onto a road by a white cottage.

⑥ Turn left and continue for about ½ mile, passing houses. Take the signposted track on the right beside a stone sign marked 'Woonsmith'.

⑦ Proceed along this track and after passing a stone bungalow on your left, take the arrowed path to the right and through a gate. Follow the stony track, passing a house and going over the moorland of Lady Downs. Cross a stone step stile beside a gate and continue along a grassy track.

⑧ At a signpost, where tracks cross, turn right following the arrow on the signpost and cross a stile into a field. Cross this field to a wooden step stile on the other side. Immediately turn right through a gate. Keeping the hedge on your left, pick up two other signposts indicating straight ahead, in the direction of fir trees, and then go through a gate and into a lane by a house. Turn right, passing Embla Farm Cottage on your left and, a little further on, Ladygate Forge, also on your left.

⑨ When reaching a road turn left and almost immediately take a footpath on the right. Go over a stile and cross a field, taking the stile on the left-hand side of a gate. Cross two fields via stiles with the hedge on your right, following the marker arrows. Continue straight ahead, negotiating four stiles, a short path and a further stile before passing cottages at Skillywadden.

⑩ At a tarmac road turn right, crossing a stream. At a T-junction turn right again and continue to the junction at Cold Harbour. Follow the signpost to St Ives.

⑪ After 350 yards take the public footpath arrowed to your right. Cross the stile and immediately go through a gate. Continue with the hedge on your left across two fields. After leaving the second field by a stile, cross a short marshy area to a wooden stile. Cross this and turn left, following the track into a lane by a house at Penderleath.

⑫ Turn left and almost immediately sharp right. After a few yards turn left over a stile and follow a path that runs beside the driveway of a house. At the end of this path enter a field over a stile, continuing through two fields keeping the hedge on your right, and straight across a third field. Leave this field on a narrow path and where you meet a cross-track with a wooden post marked 'Engine Inn', continue straight ahead and over a further two fields to the pub.

Towednack church

PLACES OF INTEREST NEARBY

The National Lighthouse Museum in Wharf Road, Penzance, provides a history of lighthouses, the men who designed them, the lives of the lighthouse keepers and a fine collection of lighthouse equipment. There is also a video theatre and a reconstructed lighthouse room. Open daily from Easter to October, 10.30 am to 4.30 pm. Telephone: 01736 360077.

Trevarrack, Lelant
The Tyringham Arms

MAP: OS EXPLORER 102
(GR 521368)

WALK 7

DISTANCE: $6\frac{1}{2}$ MILES

DIRECTIONS TO START: TURN OFF THE A30 JUST WEST OF HAYLE AND TAKE THE A3074 TOWARDS ST IVES, TURNING OFF AT THE SECOND MINI-ROUNDABOUT AND FOLLOWING THE BROWN SIGN FOR THE TYRINGHAM ARMS. THE PUB IS ABOUT $1\frac{1}{2}$ MILES ALONG THIS ROAD ON THE RIGHT. **PARKING:** THERE IS A LARGE CAR PARK FOR PATRONS, BUT PLEASE ASK PERMISSION BEFORE LEAVING YOUR CAR WHILE YOU WALK.

Our walk starts opposite the Tyringham Arms and climbs to the summit of Trencrom Hill, an Iron Age hill fort. The views extend over both coasts with St Michael's Mount and Penzance on the south coast and St Ives Bay, Godrevy lighthouse and the expanse of sands at Hayle Towans on the north coast.

From here we strike across country by lanes and paths to Knill's Monument set high above Carbis Bay. After admiring the breathtaking views we drop down to the coastal footpath at Carbis Bay, walking along the beach head and taking to the cliffs above the golden sands bordered by Atlantic rollers. Rounding the point we turn inland again and return to the Tyringham Arms by lanes and paths, emerging on a path opposite the one we left on earlier.

The Tyringham Arms

This traditional granite building was once the Trevarrack Board School and was built in 1879, closing in the mid 1960s. It became a pub and restaurant in the 1970s and takes its name from the local landowners, the Tyringham family. 'Girls and infants' is engraved in the stonework above the main door and over this hangs the old school bell. The impressive restaurant was once the school hall and has old school photographs adorning the walls. It has the air, now, of a baronial hall with its high ceilings and painted knights at the far end. The bar, once a classroom, has panelled walls, high ceilings, and an open fire in the winter. There is also a patio and children's play area.

Beers include draught Bass, Worthington, Stella Artois, Carling and Guinness and there is a comprehensive wine list, also Scrumpy Jack and Blackthorn ciders. In addition to the varied lunchtime menu, the evening menu is available all day, and there are daily specials and regular carvery nights. Fresh, tasty, home-cooked food is the priority here. Roast lunches are served every day and the house speciality is steak and ale pie, made with Guinness. Children and dogs are welcome.

Opening times in the summer are 12 noon to 2.30 pm and 6 pm to 11 pm (10.30 pm on Sundays). Food is served from 12 noon to 2.30 pm and 6 pm to 9.30 pm. Opening times in winter may vary so it is wise to ring first. Telephone: 01736 740434 or 01736 740195 (answerphone).

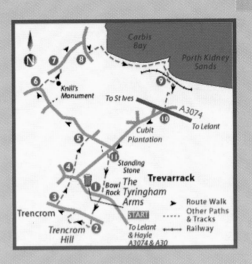

The Walk

① Leave the Tyringham Arms and turn left. After 100 yards, take the footpath on the right signposted to Trencrom. Follow the path under trees for a short distance, passing a converted chapel and going up steps beside it. Cross a stile and follow the arrows diagonally across a field and over a stile entering a road.

② Cross this, following the signs, and take the stone stile opposite. Follow the path for a short distance and turn right, climbing steadily up the slopes of Trencrom. Where the path divides go left, heading for the summit. The Iron Age Hill Fort of Trencrom Hill was given to the National Trust in 1946 by the Tyringham family, in memory of the men and women who gave their lives in the two world wars. There is an inscription on a stone at the top to commemorate this. At the top of Trencrom turn right around the granite outcrop, passing the National Trust inscription, and head in the direction of a large farm. Ignore paths to the left and right and follow the path

View of Porth Kidney Sands and Hayle Towans

along the base of the hill, dropping down to a road by way of a stile. Turn left to Trencrom hamlet.

③ Passing through the hamlet, turn right just beyond Rose Cottage and go through a metal gate. Keeping the hedge on your right, go through three fields, although the second field is very small. Cross the fourth field diagonally and go over a stile to the road.

④ Follow the public footpath sign on the opposite side of the road up a track, passing a cottage. This path goes gently uphill, leading into a road over a stile by a metal gate.

⑤ Turn left and follow this road for about a mile to where the road bends sharply left.

⑥ Take the path on the right, signposted to Knill's Monument. Where the path forks, go right. Just before the monument is a sign pointing to the left, follow this sign after having admired the magnificent views from the summit. John Knill built this monument and left money for celebrations to take place every five years. These celebrations are still held to this day, the first event taking place in 1801 in the presence of John Knill himself. Continue along this rock-strewn track, ignoring the path to the left. At the end of this track turn left and go through a gate into a lane.

⑦ Turn right and continue to the main road. Cross the road with care and turn right.

⑧ After about 100 yards turn left down Wheal Margery Lane to the coast path. The lane eventually diverts to a path on the left. Follow the yellow arrow through a metal kissing gate and continue steeply downhill. When the path meets the coastal path, turn sharp right following the arrows and stay on the path to Carbis Bay. Leave Carbis Bay by taking the road straight ahead and up the hill. Near the top of the hill, just before the railway bridge, turn left, taking the coastal footpath down steps and signposted to Lelant. Follow the path around the headland, ignoring paths to the beach.

⑨ At the end of this path turn left and immediately cross the railway line, with care, through the gates. Turn right and after 25 yards take the path up steps on your left, turning left at the end and passing houses. Follow the footpath sign across a bridge and through a kissing gate. After 20 yards turn right following the yellow arrow and take the stile by a gate. Keeping the hedge on your left, cross two fields, turning right and passing a farmhouse and going immediately left by farm buildings. At the end of this lane turn right.

⑩ When reaching the main road, cross with care and continue along the road

PLACES OF INTEREST NEARBY

The Tate Gallery at St Ives sits on the edge of Porthmeor Beach with spectacular coastal views, which would inspire any artist. This architecturally outstanding building houses changing art exhibitions selected from the Tate's collection. Opening hours are 10.30 am to 5.30 pm on Tuesday to Sunday throughout the year, also Mondays in July and August and all bank holidays (except 24-26 December). Telephone: 01736 796226.

opposite, signposted to Trevarrack. At the triangular island before the crossroads turn left and after 100 yards where this road meets another, carry straight on passing Little Trevarrack Tourist Park. Continue along this road, which has wide grass verges for quite a bit of the way, for about ½ mile.

⑪ Some 200 yards after Beersheba Farm take a stile on the left. Keep the hedge on your left and exit by a stile. Turn right and keeping the hedge on your right leave by a gate and stile onto a path, which leads down beside a cottage. Just before the road take the public footpath beside the stream and follow it to the road. The Tyringham Arms is to your right and Bowl Rock said to have been thrown there by a Cornish giant, is just around the trees to your left.

St Erth
The Star Inn

MAP: OS EXPLORER 102 (GR 551351)	**WALK 8**	DISTANCE: 5$\frac{1}{2}$ MILES

DIRECTIONS TO START: LEAVE THE A30 HAYLE TO PENZANCE ROAD AT ST ERTH STATION AND FOLLOW THE SIGNS FOR ST ERTH. **PARKING:** THERE IS A LARGE CAR PARK FOR PATRONS OF THE STAR INN, BUT PERMISSION MUST BE SOUGHT BEFORE LEAVING YOUR CAR WHILE YOU WALK.

From the Star Inn, the walk takes us along the River Hayle, which runs through the village, eventually reaching the sea at the Hayle Estuary. St Erth was, way back in time, the highest navigable point on the river. Everything about the village is unhurried. It boasts the studio and workshops of a glassblower and woodcarver while opposite the pub stands an unusual lantern cross, given to the village by Lord St Levan in 1891.

This peaceful walk begins as a leisurely amble along the river, rich in atmospheric beauty; a dragonfly skimming the water, a vivid blue butterfly, birdsong, and the wonderful red hues of the underwater weeds with the slippery forms of fish beneath the surface. At the village of Relubbus we take paths and stiles across farmland rich in plant life and luxuriant hedgerows, with distant views of St Michael's Mount, to return to St Erth.

The Star Inn

Built in 1647, the Star Inn is in the centre of the tranquil and attractive village of St Erth and stands at a crossroads on the early coaching route to Mount's Bay. Set in the roof at the back of the pub is a spy hole used to detect the customs men as they approached. The low beams are hung with a collection of brasses, three ships' lamps stand on the mantelpiece and a compass from the wreck of a French ship is set into the bar. The walls are adorned with photographs and pictures of old St Erth, together with framed collections of old postcards, the Star having won many awards for its displays of bric-a-brac. The pub has one bar, a restaurant and beer garden. Children and dogs are welcome.

Cask ales on offer include Old Speckled Hen, Flowers Original and two guest ales, one of which is usually a Cornish brew, plus over 50 malt whiskies and a good selection of wines. There is a wide range of food, with a bar menu and specials board, the emphasis being on fresh local produce, meat and fish. Cornish cream teas and an evening à la carte menu are available.

Opening times are 11 am to 11 pm (Sundays 12 noon to 10.30 pm) all through the year. Meals are served from 12 noon to 2.30 pm and from 6 pm to 9.30 pm. There is a traditional Cornish sing-along around the piano on Sunday evenings. Five en suite rooms are available, including two self-contained suites. Telephone: 01736 752068.

The Walk

① Turn left out of the pub car park and go down Chapel Hill, taking a path at the far end of the bridge on the left.

② Meander, with the River Hayle, along the valley, ignoring the two bridges and finally taking a path that runs between the river and a caravan site. After passing a wooden water wheel by a weir, turn left over a stone bridge and along a road with the river on your right. After 100 yards take the path on your right, following the river for a short distance before rejoining

PLACES OF INTEREST NEARBY

Paradise Park Wildlife Sanctuary at Hayle is a family attraction, its priority being conservation and breeding rare species. The result of this programme can be seen in the many rare birds together with otters, red pandas and red squirrels. Children will enjoy feeding the otters, penguins and parrots, and there are marvellous free-flying bird shows. Open every day at 10 am; last admissions 5 pm from May to September, 4 pm in March, April and October and 3 pm in winter. Telephone: 01736 751020.

The River Hayle

gorse bushes, to a second arrowed post. Now carry straight on and cross a stile by the gate onto the road.

⑥ We are now in Long Lanes. Turn right and proceed along this road. At the crossroads carry straight on, following the sign to St Erth. Follow Long Lanes for about a mile, ignoring the footpath sign at Trevessa Farm and the wooden stile on the right about ½ mile beyond it.

the road again. A short distance further on there is another of these 'loop paths'. Entering the village of Relubbus turn right over the bridge.

③ Turn right by the converted Methodist chapel. Continue along this lane, bearing left and passing Relubbus Vean. At the end of the lane cross a stile. Keeping the hedge on your right continue across the field. Cross another two stiles and go out onto the road.

④ Turn right, heading along the road to Trewhella Farm. Continue past the farm until the road bears right.

⑤ Take the footpath on the left, over a stile. Follow the path across the field to a direction post by a fenced mineshaft. Follow the arrow straight ahead, passing

⑦ At Tregethas Villa take the footpath through the hedge on the right. Continue with the hedge on your right and leave this field by the stile, turning left at the road. After 100 yards take the track on the right, emerging onto a road by Tredrea Manor.

⑧ Turn right, shortly passing two gateways on the right and taking the stile between high walls immediately after the second gate. Go straight ahead and follow the path heading for the village with the hedge on your right. Cross the stile and go straight across the next field to the white house. Take the stone grid beside the white house and continue into St Erth village.

Marazion
The Godolphin Arms

MAP: OS EXPLORER 102 (GR 517306)

WALK 9

DISTANCE: 5 MILES

DIRECTIONS TO START: MARAZION IS SIGNPOSTED FROM THE A394 PENZANCE TO HELSTON ROAD. **PARKING:** IN THE GODOLPHIN ARMS CAR PARK, BUT PLEASE ASK PERMISSION BEFORE LEAVING YOUR CAR WHILE YOU WALK.

Marazion is a small ancient town, or large village, tucked into the expanse of Mount's Bay and joined to St Michael's Mount by a causeway. An engraved granite stone in The Square informs us that Marazion is one of the oldest towns in the country with charters being granted in 1257 and 1595. The name comes from the Cornish, Marghas Yow, meaning Thursday Market. The Mount, owned by the National Trust, is reached by the causeway or by ferryboat, depending on the state of the tide. Either way it is an exciting adventure to spend time on this 'not quite island'. Views are magnificent with the Mount dominating the surrounding area.

The first part of the walk covers the coastal path to Perranuthnoe, over low sandstone cliffs with the rush of the sea over the rocks below, then crossing a short stretch of boulder-strewn beach which is part of the coastal footpath. At Perranuthnoe, which has several craft shops, we turn inland, along paths to the village of Goldsithney and from there across Tregurtha Downs back to Marazion.

The Godolphin Arms

This imposing Victorian building was built in the mid 1800s at a time when Marazion sought to become, as the *West Briton* of 1878 wrote, 'a watering-place'. It commands a spectacular position at the end of the causeway leading to St Michael's Mount, of which it has uninterrupted views as well as direct access to the beach, causeway and ferry. The main restaurant and bar area on the first floor has menus designed around the availability of local produce, fish, shellfish and locally grown vegetables, with an à la carte menu and daily specials. The Gig Bar, which has a terrace leading directly onto the beach, specialises in 'continental' snacks, coffee and light lunches.

There is an extensive wine list which includes an Australian wine, Angove's Misty Morning, which is made by the descendants of Cornishman Dr William Angove from Camborne, who emigrated to Australia in the 1880s. You will find a wide range of beers including local draught ales Sharp's Cornish Rebellion and Eden, and Skinner's Knocker Ale; also keg ales John Smith's and Worthington.

Opening times are 11 am to 11 pm (Sundays 12 noon to 10.30 pm). Food is served from 12 noon to 2.30 pm and 5.30 pm to 9.30 pm. Children and dogs are welcome and there is a children's indoor ball pool. Accommodation is available with ten en suite rooms, most with uninterrupted sea views. Telephone: 01736 710202.

The Walk

① Leave the Godolphin Arms and turn right, following the road for about ½ mile to the entrance of a housing estate at the other end of Marazion.

② Turn right opposite this and follow the Coastal Path sign. Follow the tarmac road and take the small path off to the left, down to the coast where the path drops down to the boulder-strewn beach. Cross this for a short distance and climb the iron steps on the other side, going up the path and over a wooden stile. Continue with the sea on your right, following the coastal footpath. Cross two consecutive stiles by some cottages and reach the road at Perranuthnoe.

③ Turn left up the hill to the village, and left again towards the church. Turn right at the T-junction, and after passing the church, turn left up a lane, which soon narrows into a path.

④ Continue along this path, bearing right, until it joins a road. Go straight on, skirting houses on your left. Cross a stile

Marazion seen from St Michael's Mount causeway

and continue through three fields keeping the hedge on your right and passing between two mineshafts. Leave by a stile and cross the corner of field 4, going over another stile into field 5. Cross this field to a stile diagonally opposite. Go over this stile, turning right. Keep the hedge on your right and leave by a stile in the hedge ahead, which leads onto the Penzance/Helston road.

⑤ Cross the road with care and take the footpath beside the gate. The village of Goldsithney is now ahead across the fields. Keep the hedge on your left and follow the field to a point where it develops into a path through high hedges and over a stile into the next field. Keeping the hedge on your left, pass through a gap in the hedge and go straight across the next field and into the village.

⑥ Turn left at the road and walk for 50 yards before taking the signposted path between houses on your right. Continue through the housing development,

PLACES OF INTEREST NEARBY

St Michael's Mount, Cornwall's fairytale castle, joined to the mainland by a causeway, dominates Mount's Bay and is a landmark for miles around. Given to the National Trust in 1954, it was originally a Benedictine priory dating back to the 12th century. It is said that the small harbour, dwarfed by the castle, could have been the site of Ictis, which exported tin around the 4th century. Open all year: between April and October, Monday to Friday, 10.30 am to 5.30 pm, last admission 4.45 pm; between November and March ring for opening details. The castle and grounds are also open most weekends during the summer for special charity days. Telephone: 01736 710507 or 710265.

St Michael's Mount

passing the cricket club on the right. Go straight ahead and through a kissing gate. Just after a bungalow turn left and immediately right, and left again at the end of this short lane along a grassy path between farm buildings.

⑦ Cross a wooden stile, turning left, and cross a field heading for the renovated mine engine house and leaving the field by a wooden stile beside a gate. At the lane turn right and continue along this track, ignoring the footpath on the left and passing the Old Counthouse on the right. Pass the riding school on the left and at the T-junction turn left.

⑧ Continue on this road, under the bypass, until you reach a crossroads by a playing field. Go straight across, passing the school on your right. Continue until you join Marazion's main street where you turn right and continue to the Godolphin Arms.

Rosudgeon
The Falmouth Packet

MAP: OS EXPLORER 102 (GR 557296) **WALK 10** DISTANCE: 5 MILES

DIRECTIONS TO START: ROSUDGEON IS SITUATED ON THE A394 BETWEEN PENZANCE AND HELSTON.
PARKING: THERE IS A PUB CAR PARK FOR PATRONS, BUT PLEASE ASK PERMISSION BEFORE LEAVING YOUR CAR WHILE YOU WALK.

From the pub the walk takes to lanes and farmland to join the coastal path as far as Kenneggy Sand. It was off this coast in 1947 that HMS *Warspite* broke loose on her way to the breakers and a heavy wooden post with metal banding used in the salvage stands on the cliffs to commemorate this. The path commands wonderful views of Mount's Bay and passes over Cudden Point and near rocky coves and bays, including Prussia Cove known for its famous son, John Carter the smuggler, who lived in the 18th century. It is easy to imagine the smuggling activity around these small rocky inlets, hidden from prying eyes, and with wheel tracks engraved in the rocks at Bessy's Cove. With none of the trappings of the present day, it is no wonder that this was one of the locations of the *Poldark* series. Soon after this we turn inland and take to lanes and footpaths, no more than ½ mile from the main road but seemingly miles from anywhere, and back to the Falmouth Packet.

The Falmouth Packet

The name of the pub comes from the Falmouth Packet sailing ships which took the mail from Cornish ports in the 16th century. The one large bar has a nautical air, as befits its name, with rope coils adorning the bar fascia and lit by replica masthead lamps. There is an extensive collection of jugs hanging from the beamed ceiling and large brass plaques adorn the chimney wall, where a coal fire burns in the winter. Outside there is a large patio area.

A good choice of food is available, including vegetarian, and there are specials boards. A roast is served every Sunday and it is advisable to book first. Traditional Cornish bitters are on offer, among them Hicks and Tinners, and a selection of house wines. Children under the age of 6 years old are not allowed in the pub at any time and those under 14 years not after 8 pm. No dogs are allowed in the bar.

Opening times, summer and winter, are 11 am to 2.30 pm and 6 pm to 11 pm, except Sundays when the hours are 12 noon to 2.30 pm and 6 pm (7 pm in winter) to 10.30 pm. Food is served at lunchtime and in the evening. The Falmouth Packet holds regular jazz nights – phone for details. Telephone: 01736 762240.

The Walk

① Leave the pub and take the road opposite, passing a sports ground on your left. Go through the hamlet of Rosudgeon, ignoring the footpath signs on either side of the road. Continue uphill and take the public footpath on your right, opposite Rosudgeon Farm.

② Follow this path and, at the end, take a stile beside the gate and keep the hedge on your left, leaving the field by another stile. Keep the hedge on your right now, going through a gate and into a lane by Acton House. Ignore the left turn here.

③ Go straight ahead, passing farm buildings, and when the lane bears left take the footpath in front of you which soon turns into a track. Continue towards the coast, passing through two gates in quick succession, followed by a third a little further on. When you reach the end of the track, turn right, heading towards St Michael's Mount. After about 100 yards turn left and immediately left again, joining the coastal footpath.

④ Follow the coastal footpath, passing the thatched fishermen's hut above Bessy's Cove and curving around Porth-en-Alls House, which stands on the edge of King's Cove.

Bessy's Cove

⑤ Pass the row of old coastguard cottages, and after 50 yards a quarry, after which you pass through a wooden gate. After a further 50 yards take the path on the left, above Kenneggy Sand, climbing steadily inland. Shortly after you pass a ruined building, paths meet. Turn left and when the path joins a lane, continue straight ahead. This lane becomes a tarmac lane as it passes the farm at Higher Kenneggy. Continue straight ahead to the crossroads on the Penzance to Helston road.

⑥ Cross the road and take the lane opposite. Where the lanes cross continue straight ahead.

⑦ When the lanes cross again, turn left. After about 300 yards the lane narrows into a path. Continue for about 400 yards and soon after passing a house on your left, turn left along a short path, joining a lane. Continue along this lane into Packet Lane.

⑧ Turn left. At the main road turn left to the pub.

PLACES OF INTEREST NEARBY

Trevarno Gardens, north-west of Helston, are described as 'An historic and tranquil haven protected and unspoilt for 700 years'. The Victorian and Georgian gardens contain a large collection of rare shrubs and trees, and there are woodland walks and walled gardens. There is also a gardening museum with a fascinating collection of tools and implements. Open from 10.30 am to 5 pm all year round. Telephone: 01326 574274.

Godolphin Cross
The Godolphin Arms

MAP: OS EXPLORER 102
(GR 609312)

WALK 11

DISTANCE: 6$\frac{1}{2}$ MILES

DIRECTIONS TO START: GODOLPHIN CROSS IS SIGNPOSTED FROM TOWNSHEND ON THE B3280 LEEDSTOWN TO MARAZION ROAD. **PARKING:** THERE IS PARKING FOR PATRONS AT THE GODOLPHIN ARMS, BUT PLEASE ASK PERMISSION BEFORE YOU LEAVE YOUR CAR WHILE YOU WALK.

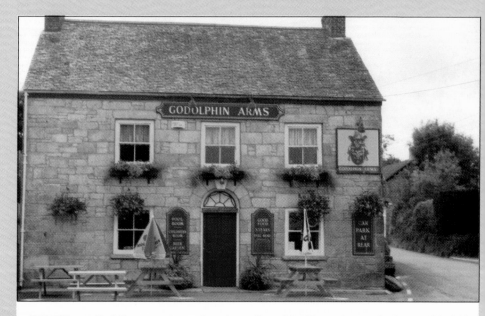

The walk follows tracks and paths, with the recommended option of climbing to the top of Tregonning Hill where the war memorial to the men of St Germoe in the form of a Cornish Cross mounted on a three tier plinth dominates the surrounding moorland countryside. The area by the trig point is Castle Pencaire (fort). There are panoramic views across Mount's Bay and St Michael's Mount to the south and the Penwith hills to the north. Cornwall is laid out like a map below us, a patchwork of earth colours and contrasting greens, with the sea a splash of blue across the horizon. We descend Tregonning Hill, passing the hamlet of Balwest, and take to paths and lanes passing Godolphin Hill and Godolphin Warren, which belong to the National Trust. The return to the village of Godolphin Cross is by a woodland walk beside Godolphin House.

The Godolphin Arms

The Godolphin Arms is at the centre of the village of Godolphin Cross and was built of Cornish granite with a mounting block on one wall, in the early 1800s. We were told that a pub of this name was originally sited at Trewithen Terrace, nearby, but moved into the present building when the local mines closed. The unusual shaped bar, with its low, beamed ceiling and natural stone walls, has a warm, friendly feel about it. As well as the bar there is a dining room and additional eating area, a beer garden, a children's room and a play area. Dogs are welcome too. A full menu is on offer and the Godolphin Arms has a wide reputation for its steaks. The beers include Sharp's real ales, Cornish Doom Bar and Coaster. A list of wines is available, plus house wines.

Summer opening times are 12 noon to 2.30 pm and 6 pm to 11 pm, with food being served from 12 noon to 2 pm and 6 pm to 9.30 pm. Winter times are 12 noon to 2 pm and 6.30 pm to 11 pm with food being served from 12 noon to 2 pm and from 6.30 pm to 9.30 pm. Sunday opening is from 12 noon to 3 pm and 6.30 pm to 10.30 pm all the year with food served at lunchtime and in the evening. Telephone: 01736 762879 during pub opening times.

The Walk

① Leave the pub car park and turn left, passing the school on your right and the churchyard on your left. Continue along

this country road, following the signs to Ashton, for about 1¼ miles until reaching the hamlet of Balwest.

② Turn left, following a public footpath sign by a seat. Continue up the hill. Where the track levels out is a track to the left. Here there is the highly recommended option of climbing to the top of Tregonning Hill (up and back on the same track), where there is a 360° panoramic view of West Cornwall laid out before you. Otherwise continue along the track. At a cross-track, carry straight on along a narrow path, heading for a white house.

③ Just before the gate to the house follow the yellow arrowed post, taking the footpath on the right and going over a stile into a field. Follow the path straight ahead down the field, keeping the hedge on your right. Cross a wooden stile at the end of this field and proceed along a grassy path, between high hedges. Leave the path over a stile beside a gate, into a lane. Continue straight ahead along the lane to a road.

The war memorial on Tregonning Hill

④ Turn right and follow this road along to Balwest, ignoring the left turn to Tresowes Green.

⑤ Turn left at the road junction by Balwest Cottage following the signpost to Germoe. Ignore the public footpath sign soon after this.

⑥ After Lower Balwest Farm, turn right along a grassy track. After 200 yards the track bears right; take the path straight ahead. Cross a stile and continue into a lane, turning right. Continue along this lane, joining the road.

⑦ Turn left and continue along the road, then take the first turn on the left, following a signpost for Boscrege, and pass a caravan site on your left. Follow the road as it bears right by Rose Cottage, emerging onto another road by a telephone box.

⑧ Turn left and after 50 yards turn right along Rocky Lane. Follow Rocky Lane for about a mile with Godolphin Warren and Hill on your right.

PLACES OF INTEREST NEARBY

Godolphin House is a Tudor and Stuart grade 1 mansion incorporating a side garden dating back to 1320 and an informal museum of horse-drawn farm implements. There is an exhibition of features saved from the historic Red Lion Hotel in Truro, which was demolished in 1968. Open on Thursday and Sunday from May to September, Fridays also from July to September and all Bank Holiday Mondays from Easter to August, 2 pm to 5 pm. Telephone: 01736 763194.

Godolphin Hill

⑨ At the end of Rocky Lane turn right along the road and continue for approximately ½ mile, before taking a National Trust path over a wooden stile on your right.

⑩ Follow the path through woodland and after about ½ mile, where the track bends to the left to further woodland, take the path signposted on the right through the hedge and over a stile. Follow the path straight ahead over grassland. Exit by a stile through a hedge and continue straight ahead through the woods, passing the buildings of Godolphin House. Godolphin House is privately owned but open to the public and was used as a location for the *Poldark* television series and, more recently, *Frenchman's Creek*. Leave the woods over a stile, entering a field and keeping the hedge on your right. Ahead is Godolphin Cross. Go through the gate, crossing the next field diagonally.

⑪ Turn left on a woodland path beside a stream. After 20 yards go over a stile on the right and immediately cross the stream by stepping stones, continuing up steps on the other side. Turn left along a lane, and right at the road to Godolphin Cross.

Gweek
The Gweek Inn

| MAP: OS EXPLORER 103 (GR 707268) | WALK 12 | DISTANCE: 3½ MILES |

DIRECTIONS TO START: TAKE THE A3083 HELSTON/LIZARD ROAD AND FOLLOW THE SIGNS FOR GWEEK AT THE MINI-ROUNDABOUT JUST AFTER RNAS CULDROSE. **PARKING:** THERE IS PARKING FOR PATRONS IN THE PUB CAR PARK, BUT PLEASE ASK PERMISSION BEFORE LEAVING YOUR CAR WHILE YOU WALK.

There are three sides to Gweek on the Helford River. Look one way and it is a village on a wooded, tidal creek, with boating interests and once a very busy port, with large ships using the waterway with ease. Look the other way and it is a little country village amidst rolling farmland, with whitewashed cottages, granite cottages and roses around the door type cottages. Look the third way and, although it is well hidden, there lies the National Seal Sanctuary. Sitting on the village 'green' beside the creek you wouldn't know it was there. Gweek has a feel of community about it with its pub, tearooms, shop/post office, reading room, and notice board advertising, amongst other things, the long established Gweek Silver Band.

Leaving the creekside our walk takes us through rolling farmland following paths and bridleways. The hedgerows were abundant with foliage and wildflowers scented the air when we were there. You will have distant views of Goonhilly Earth Station, RNAS Culdrose and a wind farm en route.

The Gweek Inn

This 19th century traditional Cornish inn stands close to the creekside, in the centre of the village. It has had several name changes during its history, originally being the Gweek Hotel, then the Gweek Inn, followed by the Black Swan and it is now, once again, the Gweek Inn. There is one large, airy bar with beamed ceilings, natural stone walls and real fires on cold days. The walls are adorned with photographs of shipwrecks, a framed collection of nautical knots and there is a display of model aeroplanes. The inn has a non-smoking dining room, a terrace area and a beer garden.

Real ales on offer are Wadworth 6X, Old Speckled Hen, Bass, Director's, Flowers IPA and a guest ale, together with a full range of wines. There is an extensive menu, which is the same throughout, in the restaurant and in the bar, plus daily specials. The emphasis is on home-cooked food using the best ingredients, together with local fish and produce. Children, and dogs on leads, are welcome.

Opening times in the winter are 12 noon to 2.30 pm and 6.30 pm to 11 pm; Sundays 12 noon to 2.30 pm and 7 pm to 10.30 pm. Food is served from 12 noon to 2 pm and 6.30 pm (Sundays 7 pm) to 9 pm. Summer opening times are 11.30 am to 3 pm and 6 pm to 11 pm; Sundays 12 noon to 3 pm and 7 pm to 10.30 pm. Food is served from 12 noon to 2.30 pm and 6.30 pm (Sundays 7 pm) to 9.30 pm. Telephone: 01326 221502.

The Walk

① Leave the inn and turn left, crossing the bridge. Follow the road out of Gweek for about ¼ mile and after a second bridge turn right, following a public footpath sign opposite the road to Lower Quay.

② Follow this narrow lane across the river over a flat stone bridge, passing cottages, to the end where a stile leads into a field. Keep the hedge on your right and cross this field and the next, going through a metal gate into the third field. Turn left, and now keeping the hedge on your left,

PLACES OF INTEREST NEARBY

The National Seal Sanctuary at Gweek was established more than 40 years ago and is Europe's leading marine animal rescue centre caring for dozens of sick, injured and orphaned seals. Their aim is to return all these pups back into the wild. The visitor can become a temporary member of the Animal Care Team and experience what a seal pup rescue is really like. Gift shop and café. Open from 9 am daily; last admission 5 pm. Winter opening times may differ. Telephone: 01326 221874.

Gweek Quay

continue around two sides of this field and into the next, crossing this also with the hedge on your left. At the end of this field follow a yellow arrowed signpost to the left under trees, over a wooden bridge and through a kissing gate beside a lake. Skirt the lake, keeping it on your left and on reaching the hedge keep this on your left also. Exit this field by a metal gate onto a track. Follow this track through Pollard Mill and on reaching a road turn right.

③ Continue along this road until you see a public bridleway signpost on your right (at this point the road veers to the left).

④ Follow this bridleway straight ahead for about ¼ mile and where the track forks, go left and continue straight ahead for a further ½ mile.

⑤ At the road turn right and head downhill to Gweek.

Gunwalloe
The Halzephron Inn

MAP: OS EXPLORER 103
(GR 657225)

WALK 13

DISTANCE: $3\frac{1}{2}$ OR 8 MILES

DIRECTIONS TO START: TAKE THE A3083 HELSTON/LIZARD ROAD, TURNING OFF SOUTH-WEST (JUST AFTER THE BRIDGE CROSSING THE ROAD AT RNAS CULDROSE IF APPROACHING FROM HELSTON), SIGNPOSTED TO GUNWALLOE. **PARKING:** THERE IS PARKING FOR PATRONS AT THE HALZEPHRON INN, BUT PLEASE ASK PERMISSION BEFORE YOU LEAVE YOUR CAR WHILE YOU WALK.

This walk begins above the shingle beach of Gunwalloe Fishing Cove with distant views over Mount's Bay and the Land's End peninsula. We take country paths, abundant with wildflowers and birdsong, down to Carminowe Creek, joining with Loe Pool, Cornwall's largest natural lake, and circling it on the woodland paths of the Penrose Estate, owned by the National Trust. Loe Bar forms a natural barrier between the fresh water of the pool and the salt water of the sea. There are danger notices here and at Gunwalloe Fishing Cove, advising of the strong currents and deep water and warning not to enter the sea or Loe Pool at any time. After crossing the Bar we take to the coastal footpath, passing the memorial on the cliffs. We follow the coastal path to Gunwalloe Fishing Cove and back to the Halzephron Inn.

The Halzephron Inn

This immensely popular inn is close to the coastal footpath at Gunwalloe. Built 500 years ago, it is thought to have been the haunt of smugglers and has a shaft connecting it to an underground tunnel. Formerly called the Ship it was delicensed in the early 1900s and remained so until 1958 when the licence was reinstated. The name Halzephron comes from the old Cornish 'Als Yfferin', meaning cliffs of hell, a reference to the many wrecks in this area. The main bar area has low, beamed ceilings, various eating corners leading from it and there is a 'bistro' style restaurant and large family room. There are attractive patio areas at the front and back. Dogs are allowed outside only.

The menu offers an excellent range of food, including a children's menu, the emphasis being on fresh local produce. There are also speciality cheeses available, among them Cornish Yarg and Cornish Brie. Real ales on offer include a choice of Cornish brews, also a large selection of malt whiskies, wines, spirits and liqueurs.

Opening times are 11 am to 2.30 pm and 6 pm (6.30 pm in winter) to 11 pm; Sundays 12 noon to 2.30 pm and 6 pm (7 pm in winter) to 10.30 pm. Food is served from 12 noon to 2 pm and 6.30 pm to 9.30 pm (7 pm to 9 pm in winter). There is overnight accommodation in the form of two double en suite bedrooms. Telephone: 01326 240406.

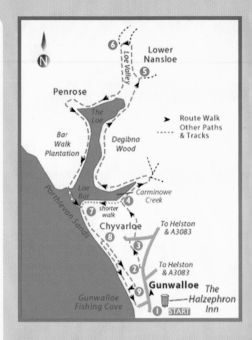

The Walk

① Leave the Halzephron Inn and turn right. When you reach a children's playground on the left, take the road on the left, opposite a post box.

② After about 200 yards look for a signposted path through the hedge on the left into a field. Exit this field by a stile near the opposite right-hand corner, about 20 yards to the left of a gate. Leave the second field by a stile in the opposite hedge. Keeping the hedge on your right leave the third field through a gate onto a track, and follow this track, entering a lane at Chyvarloe.

③ Turn right and after about 100 yards take the path over a stile on the left just before farm buildings. Keep the hedge on your right and head for a wooden stile beside a gate and into a grassy lane and continue down this woodland path. Exit

Loe Bar and the coastal footpath

the woods through a gate and continue through two more gates to Carminowe Creek.

④ The walk can be shortened here by turning left, taking the path to Loe Bar (point 7) and returning to the Halzephron by the coastal footpath. For the main walk, turn right and follow the creek, crossing a boardwalk at the head of the creek and passing a sign for Degibna. Turn left around the creek head and continue following the creek, passing Lower Pentire Barn where the path develops into a track. About 200 yards after this take the narrow path on the left, which leads into a field. A little further along here Carminowe Creek joins with Loe Pool. Continue along the banks of the pool. Turn right by a seat and, keeping the hedge on your left, continue through a kissing gate. Follow the woodland path through Degibna Wood beside Loe Pool for about 1½ miles. Pass through another kissing gate and continue beside Loe Pool, following a sign for Helston. On leaving the pool

PLACES OF INTEREST NEARBY

Halzephron Herb Farm (within sight of the Halzephron Inn) is situated on the cliffs overlooking Mount's Bay. It offers a wide range of home-grown fresh young herb plants, home-made marinades, salad dressings, chutneys, dips, jams, honey, herbal medicines and much, much more. The Pet's Corner, tennis court, mini football pitch and play area are all free to customers. Open on Monday to Saturday: 11 am to 4 pm from February to June and October to Christmas Eve; 10 am to 6 pm from July to September. Telephone: 01326 240652.

Loe Pool

behind, go through a field before reaching a concrete road near Lower Nansloe Farm.

⑤ Turn left. After about 200 yards, just before the ruins of a mine engine house, turn left and go through a National Trust gate on a path that crosses a bridge and causeway.

⑥ When this joins the main path through Penrose Estate, turn left. When the road forks turn left, following a signpost for Loe Bar. Continue for about 1¼ miles before reaching the coast, and turning left to cross Loe Bar.

⑦ After crossing Loe Bar, take the coastal footpath with the memorial on your right.

This memorial is in memory of about 100 officers and men of HMS *Anson* who were drowned when the ship was wrecked here in 1807. As a result of this, Henry Trengrouse of Helston invented the lifesaving rocket apparatus. After about 400 yards the path divides.

⑧ Take the upper path (there is a lower path but this passes close to the cliff edge).

⑨ After about ½ mile take the path on the right between two granite gate posts, just before a viewpoint seat. At the coast, turn left and follow the coastal path to Gunwalloe Fishing Cove. Turn left and continue up the lane to the pub.

The Lizard
The Top House

MAP: OS EXPLORER 103
(GR 703125)

WALK 14

DISTANCE: 3, 5 OR 8 MILES

DIRECTIONS TO START: TAKE THE A3083 FROM HELSTON TO LIZARD VILLAGE. **PARKING:** OUTSIDE THE PUB OR IN THE LARGE FREE CAR PARK IN THE CENTRE OF THE VILLAGE WITH AN HONESTY BOX.

The Lizard is the most southerly point in England and there is the most southerly café and the most southerly house to prove it. Our route circles Lizard Village walking along hedge top paths, giving a marvellous feeling of the world at your feet!

We follow inland paths to join the coastal footpath just before Cadgwith, where we turn towards the Lizard, passing through the National Trust village of Church Cove. Wonderful sea views all around with the sea at the Lizard bubbling and boiling around the offshore rocks. Watch out for seals here; we saw three. Some of the stone used in the stiles in this area is the local stone, serpentine, which gets very smooth with wear. This can make them slippery especially in wet weather. You can watch serpentine stone being worked here and made into ornaments. The full walk continues along the coastal footpath to the National Trust car park above Kynance Cove, where we turn back to Lizard Village and the end of the walk.

The Top House

Cornwall's most southerly pub was originally a farmhouse then a coaching inn, and has been licensed for nearly 200 years. Before 1951 it was known as Hill's Hotel, and later the Lizard Hotel, before acquiring its present name in 1986. There were, at one time, two pubs in the village, the Top House being on slightly higher ground hence its name.

This is a village pub with a warm and welcoming atmosphere and excellent food. There is one large bar, designated areas for children and non-smokers, plus an outside seating area for the summer. Dogs are welcome. Hot and cold meals are served at lunchtimes and in the evenings throughout the year, and there are specials boards, vegetarian dishes and a children's menu. Beers on offer are Banks's Mild and Sharp's Doom Bar and there is an extensive wine list.

Opening times are 11 am to 11 pm; Sundays 12 noon to 10.30 pm. Food is served from 12 noon to 2.30 pm and 6.30 pm to 9 pm every day. Telephone: 01326 290974.

The Walk

① Leave the pub and take the road opposite, which is Beacon Terrace, following this road, passing the school and bearing left. Keep bearing left and follow the signpost for Helston.

② About 200 yards after this the road does a sharp left-hand bend; ignore this and go straight on, taking the public footpath over a stone stile, signposted to Cadgwith. Follow the track beside the field and exit by another stile on your right. Now keeping the hedge on your left continue over two more fields before leaving over a stone stile beside a metal gate into a lane. Continue straight ahead and at the farm turn right, taking the footpath for Cadgwith and Ruan Minor. Take a step stile beside a gate, following the footpath along the top of the hedge, with views of Goonhilly Earth Station ahead. This path meanders above the fields for about 400 yards before crossing a field and exiting over a stile beside a metal gate and following the track to the road.

③ Turn right, and after about 400 yards, where the road bends to the left, take the footpath signposted on your right. This heads towards the coast. After 200 yards take the footpath signposted on your right leading to the coast path. After about 100 yards this meets the coastal path.

④ Turn right over a stile and continue to Church Cove.

Church Cove

⑤ At this point, if you want to shorten the walk, turn right to return to Lizard Village. Otherwise, to continue the walk, turn left downhill, and take the coastal path to the right, passing the lifeboat station at Kilcobben Cove. Continue on the coastal footpath to the Lizard, where, again, the walk can be shortened by taking the lane directly to Lizard Village.

⑥ Otherwise, pass above the old lifeboat station at Polpeor Cove and eventually leave the coastal footpath at the National Trust car park above Kynance Cove. If time permits, Kynance Cove is well worth a visit to see its unusual rock formations.

⑦ At the car park turn right and follow the toll road for about ½ mile, where it bears left, after a bungalow.

⑧ Leave the road here and continue straight on over a stone stile following the footpath sign. This path continues straight across the fields heading for Lizard Village, eventually developing into another hedge top path that takes you right back into the village centre.

PLACES OF INTEREST NEARBY

Goonhilly Earth Station, on Goonhilly Downs south of Helston, is the largest Satellite Earth Station in the world and has probably transmitted and received more world events than any other. Visitors can experience a guided tour of the complex, take part in interactive displays and visit the multimedia visitors' centre, amongst other attractions. Open daily from late March to October, 10 am to 5 pm – or 6 pm depending on the season. Telephone: 0800 679 593.

Stithians
The Seven Stars Inn

MAP: OS EXPLORER 104 (GR 733370)	WALK 15	DISTANCE: 3½ MILES

DIRECTIONS TO START: TURN SOUTH-EAST OFF THE B3297 REDRUTH TO HELSTON ROAD, FOLLOWING THE SIGNS FOR STITHIANS. **PARKING:** THERE IS AMPLE ROADSIDE PARKING BY THE PUB.

The footpaths around Stithians are wonderful, a walkers' delight! They are many, well-marked and, on the whole, clearly visible. One path is actually paved right across the field! Stithians is a very active village just outside Redruth and is the home of the Stithian's Agricultural Show, an annual one day show in July each year, which was first held in 1834, a Silver Band and both a ladies' choir and a male voice choir. There is also the Stithians Local History Group, which regularly publishes books on the various aspects of village history and a CD-ROM recording life in the village at the turn of the Millennium.

Our walk circles the village on country paths until we reach the shores of Stithians Reservoir, which is reputedly the windiest inland water in England. After following the lake for a while, we turn inland and once again follow the marvellous footpaths of Stithians before arriving back in the village.

The Seven Stars Inn

You will get a warm village welcome at the Seven Stars Inn in the centre of Stithians. Even the slate flagstone floors welcome walkers, with no worries about muddy walking boots! Relax and enjoy the hospitality of a real country local where everyone is ready to make you part of their village for as long as you want to stay. Children and dogs are welcome too. The pub was originally built by a farmer who owned Ennis and Carbis Farm, which adjoins it. The open plan bar area has low, beamed ceilings and granite fireplaces, and is decorated with old photographs of the pub and mining scenes, and there is a beer garden at the rear.

Beers on offer are Skinner's and Sharp's and a guest ale. In addition to the main menu there are daily lunchtime specials, and in the evening a chef's special.

Weekday opening times are 12 noon to 3 pm and 7 pm (6 pm on Fridays) to 11 pm; Saturdays 11 am to 11 pm; Sundays 12 noon to 10.30 pm (closed from 3.30 pm to 7 pm in winter). Food is served from 12 noon to 2 pm and 7 pm to 9 pm and is available on Wednesday to Sunday and at lunchtime on Mondays. Telephone: 01209 860003.

The Walk

① Leave the inn and turn right, heading for the church and taking the road on the left, signposted to Redruth, Hendra Road.

② On reaching a lane on the right, cross the stile and follow the footpath. When you come to a stile showing a paved path across a field beyond it, ignore this, turning left and keeping the hedge on your right. Go over an arrowed step stile and, keeping the hedge on your right cross four fields via stiles until you come to a lane. Cross the lane and take the stile opposite, crossing this field to a stile in line with the Fourlanes television mast. Now keep the hedge on your right and cross a stile into the next field, proceeding with the hedge on your left. Cross a stile by a metal gate onto a track at Treskewis Farm.

③ Turn left, passing the farm buildings, and where the track divides turn left to a metal gate and take the stile on your right. Cross two fields, keeping the hedge on your left. Leave this field by a stile onto a woodland path. Follow this path, taking the right-hand fork and passing between cottages into the village of Goonlaze.

④ Take the road opposite, and after about ½ mile turn left at Tresevern House and follow the path that runs beside Stithians Reservoir. Continue to the end of this

Stithians Reservoir

path, with the car park on your right, then entering a road. Turn left and proceed along the road for about ¼ mile.

⑤ Just after a white house, where the road bears left by some stables, take the lane on your right and almost immediately cross a stile on your left, exiting this field by a stile diagonally across the field in line with Stithians church. Cross three fields via stiles and after negotiating a stepped stile over a hedge, head for a stile diagonally across the field, in the top left-hand corner. The path crosses two fields leading to bungalows and goes between them, entering a lane.

⑥ Turn downhill and into the village.

PLACES OF INTEREST NEARBY

Poldark Mine at Wendron, on the B3297 north of Helston, is a genuine 18th century tin mine, unworked since about 1820. It gives the visitor a chance to see the working conditions of Cornwall's miners of that time on guided underground tours. The museum contains reminders recovered from a 25 year programme of excavations. There is plenty to do for all the family and they warn you to allow at least 4 hours. Open all year from 10 am to 6 pm; last mine tour 4 pm. Telephone: 01326 573173.

Piece
The Countryman

MAP: OS EXPLORER 104 (GR 679398)	**WALK 16**	DISTANCE: 4 OR 5 MILES

DIRECTIONS TO START: PIECE IS WEST OF THE B3297 REDRUTH/HELSTON ROAD. APPROACHING FROM REDRUTH, TAKE THE FIRST TURN TO THE RIGHT SIGNPOSTED TO CARNKIE. THE COUNTRYMAN STANDS ON A T-JUNCTION ABOUT A MILE AFTER THE VILLAGE OF CARNKIE. **PARKING:** THERE IS A PUB CAR PARK FOR PATRONS, BUT PERMISSION MUST BE ASKED BEFORE LEAVING YOUR CAR WHILE YOU WALK.

The walk starts over farmland and then climbs the slopes of Carn Brea, an ancient hilltop fortress, dominating the towns of Redruth and Camborne, which can be seen for many miles around. This is an inland walk but with distant panoramic coastal views. Strange shaped rocks lie around on Carn Brea, piled high and sculptured by the weather. Carn Brea Castle is actually built precariously on these rock piles.

Walking the length of the ridge we drop down into a country lane and then follow the Great Flat Lode mining trail through a landscape of derelict mine buildings, once so busy but now a silent memorial to the men who worked them. At Samson's Shaft the path divides and it is possible to shorten the walk here. However, we recommend that you go on, passing through the Basset Mines Tramway Tunnel.

The Countryman

Formerly called the Pendarves Arms, the Countryman is about 150 years old. The saloon bar was once the count house where wages were paid to the local miners, and an alehouse. The ghosts of three bal maidens are said to be present at the inn. Bal maidens were surface workers at the many mines in Cornwall in the heyday of the industry and many would have been employed at the mines on our walk. The lounge bar has an old Cornish range set into one of the natural stone walls, which are the original walls of the cottage that stood beside the count house and alehouse. There are the two bar areas, lounge and saloon, a pool room, a garden with tables and a verandah.

Over 20 beers and lagers are on offer, including eight real ales, three of which are brewed locally. One of these, No Name, is brewed exclusively for the Countryman Inns. There is a varied wine list including house wines. A comprehensive menu, much of which is home-made, includes vegetarian and children's meals. Cornish pasties are baked on the premises and chef's specials are offered daily. Well-behaved children and dogs are welcome everywhere except the lounge bar.

Opening times are 11 am to 11 pm on Monday to Saturday and 12 noon to 10.30 pm on Sunday. Food is served from 11 am to 10 pm on Monday to Saturday and 12 noon to 10 pm on Sunday. Telephone: 01209 215960.

The Walk

① Leave the pub, turn left and immediately left again, over a stile beside the pub. Keeping the hedge on your left, cross the field and go over a stile into the next field. Continue straight across this field, passing close to mine waste on your right, and cross another stile into a lane.

② Turn left and after 20 yards take the path on your right, crossing a low stile followed by a stile into a field. Head diagonally across this field to another stile leading into a lane by a large black barn. Turn right.

③ After 100 yards turn right again. Shortly the lane develops into a path. Take this path which heads for the top of Carn Brea. On reaching the summit make for the monument, which is in memory of Lord de Dunstanville of Tehidy. Follow the path to the castle and on passing the castle take the path straight ahead. Follow this path for 50 yards before turning right and taking the downward path to the valley. Where the path divides, take the right-hand fork. This path meanders

Carn Brea

downhill for about ¼ mile before coming to a place where five paths meet.

④ Take the path diagonally ahead, heading for the TV mast. The path leads into a lane by three cottages on your right. Take the next left, following the Great Flat Lode trail.

⑤ At the road in Church Coombe, turn left and follow the road for about ⅓ mile.

⑥ At Coombe Gardens turn sharp right, following the Great Flat Lode trail. At the fork, turn right and continue, ignoring the paths to the mines.

⑦ At the road, cross with care, taking the road opposite. After 100 yards turn right, continuing through a gate. Continue on this track for about a mile, ignoring all

paths to left and right and passing various mine buildings and capped mineshafts en route.

⑧ At Samson's Shaft the path divides and it is possible to shorten the walk here by taking the left-hand path onto the road and turning right, back to the

PLACES OF INTEREST NEARBY

At **Cornwall's Industrial Discovery Centre** (Pool, west of Redruth) there are two Cornish beam engine houses with their engines intact. The visitor will discover how these engine houses operated when they either pumped the mines dry or carried men and materials up and down the shaft. Open from April to October on Sunday to Friday plus Bank Holiday Saturdays, 11 am to 5 pm. Telephone for winter opening details: 01209 315027.

Basset Mines Tramway Tunnel

Countryman. To continue, take the right-hand path, passing Samson's Shaft and going through the Basset Mines Tramway Tunnel. The tunnel was built in 1908 and rebuilt in 1997, and some of the finest examples of mine buildings in Cornwall's mining heritage, are just a little further along. Passing through a wooden barrier, cross a road and go straight on along the track, bearing left. Pass a car park on the left and go straight on towards the mine buildings. Go through a wooden barrier, turn right and head for the mine buildings. Taking the right-hand path, skirt the buildings. At the end of the track turn right and continue for 50 yards, turning left, heading for two further mines. Take the right-hand path to skirt the first engine house. After the second one turn right to the gate at the end of the gravel path. Go through the wooden barrier.

⑨ Turn right in the hamlet of Treskillard. After ¼ mile turn right at the road junction to return to the Countryman.

Portreath
The Basset Arms

MAP: OS EXPLORER 104 (GR 654452)	WALK 17	DISTANCE: 2 OR 3 MILES

DIRECTIONS TO START: PORTREATH IS ON THE B3300, AND IS ON THE COAST ABOUT 4 MILES FROM REDRUTH. **PARKING:** IN THE SEAFRONT CAR PARK NEARBY, PLUS AMPLE ROADSIDE PARKING.

Our walk circles the village of Portreath on the north coast, which was once a very important port, connected to Cornish tin mining. Coal was imported from South Wales for the pumping engines at the mines and a tramroad was built to connect the port with the mines inland. The harbour has a very narrow entrance bordered by the harbour wall on one side and towering cliffs on the other.

We cross the harbour area, taking the coastal path for a short way to the east, then dropping back into the valley by a path that runs almost the length of the village. Wonderful views all around. We cross the road and climb out of the village to the west. Here there is the option to shorten the walk to 2 miles. The full walk continues over farmland to join the road for a short distance. We then follow a lane high above Portreath, once more, and descend close to the Basset Arms.

The Basset Arms

Situated close to the beach, the Basset Arms has had close associations with the sea and seafarers throughout its history. Old photographs of Portreath decorate the walls and a framed series of newspaper cuttings tell the story of one of Portreath's wrecks, the SS *Escurial*, en route between Cardiff and the Adriatic, that took place in 1895. Some survivors of the wreck were tended here and the inquest into the deaths of the second mate and carpenter was held in the pub. Those drowned were laid out in an outbuilding of the pub.

This is a traditional Cornish local with low, beamed ceilings and very friendly atmosphere. There is one bar and a non-smoking dining room. Beers on offer include the local real ale Sharp's Doom Bar, also Theakston and Courage Best, but these are subject to change. There is a full wine list. The menu is extensive and in addition there is a specials board. A speciality is the fully inclusive evening meal where the price of the main course includes unlimited starters, desserts, coffee and cola or lemonade for the children. There is also a children's play area. Dogs are allowed in the conservatory.

Summer opening is 11 am to 11 pm; Sundays 12 noon to 10.30 pm. Winter is 11.30 am to 2.30 pm and 6 pm to 11 pm; Sundays 12 noon to 10.30 pm. Food is served from 12 noon to 2 pm and 6.30 pm to 9.30 pm. Telephone: 01209 842077.

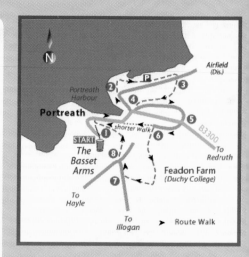

The Walk

① Outside the pub, take the bridge over the stream and cross the main road, turning right. Turn left into Forth an Nance and head for the harbour. Turn right and follow the harbourside. On reaching the harbour head turn left through railings and follow the harbour seaward on the opposite side. When reaching the information board turn sharp right up a short lane and then left into Lighthouse Hill and continue steeply upwards.

② Soon after the hairpin bend follow the acorn sign to the left and onto the coastal path. After passing a car park turn right, and then left on reaching the road.

PLACES OF INTEREST NEARBY

Tehidy Country Park, south-west of Portreath, covers 250 acres close to the cliffs on the north coast and includes over 9 miles of woodland, lake and riverside paths, once being part of the estate of the mine owning family, the Bassets. Open all year. Telephone: 01209 714494.

Portreath

returning directly to the Basset Arms.

⑥ For the full walk, pass the castle, ignoring the footpath sign on your right, and continue up the hill, which soon leads onto a woodland path. Follow the path to Duchy College Farm. At the end of this path turn right, heading towards chalets. At the T-junction turn left and then right after 50 yards, along a wide stony track. After 200 yards we pass across the track bed of the incline railway which can be seen to left and right. Walk a further 100 yards and take the stile on the right, going straight across the field to a stile in the opposite hedge. Keeping the hedge on your left, head for a stile that leads onto a road.

③ After 150 yards turn right down a grassy lane. This path will lead you high above Portreath and back to Lighthouse Hill and gives a bird's eye view of the village and, towards the end of the path, a fine view of the mineral tramway incline across the valley.

④ Turn left down Lighthouse Hill and left again immediately after the Portreath Arms and along Sunnyvale Road. Continue to the end, emerging onto the road opposite Portreath School.

⑤ Cross the road and turn right, taking the road down beside the school. After 50 yards, bear right and continue along this road until it veers left leading to a small castle, Glenfeaden Castle. It is at this point that the walk can be shortened by

⑦ Turn right and continue on this road for 200 yards, taking care at the triangular road junction and heading for Green Lane, straight ahead.

⑧ This lane narrows after ¼ mile into a path leading downwards. Turn left at the bottom of the steps and immediately right and into the village.

St Agnes
The Railway Inn

DIRECTIONS TO START: TURN OFF THE A30 APPROXIMATELY 3 MILES EAST OF REDRUTH, AT THE CHYVERTON ROUNDABOUT, AND TAKE THE B3277, FOLLOWING SIGNS TO ST AGNES.
PARKING: THE RAILWAY INN HAS A CAR PARK FOR PATRONS, BUT PERMISSION MUST BE SOUGHT BEFORE LEAVING YOUR CAR WHILE YOU WALK. THERE IS A FREE PUBLIC CAR PARK NEXT DOOR.

The Railway Inn is in the centre of St Agnes and the walk takes us through the village, which was once the centre of intensive mining activity. Engine houses of the mines dominate the landscape. Two of these are actually sited within the village and modern houses have grown up around them. As we leave the village, panoramic views of the coast open up and we walk a section of the coastal footpath as far as Wheal Coates engine house. Care must be taken to keep to the footpaths as this area has been heavily mined; proof of which can be seen in the capped mine shafts and engine houses en route. We then turn inland, following paths to St Agnes Beacon, which stands high above the village and has magnificent views on all sides. It is said that 31 church towers can be seen from here on a good day. From here we drop down into St Agnes, emerging within a few yards of the pub.

The Railway Inn

This is a traditional oak-beamed pub, over 300 years old. Originally named the Smith Arms because of the blacksmith's shop nearby, it was re-named when the railway came to St Agnes in the early 1900s. The Railway has a ghost in the form of Dorcas who threw herself down a nearby mine when her fiancé was killed in a mining accident. When she passes through the inn, the third lamp on the bar sways. It is said that her ghost saved the life of a miner by warning him to get away before a rock fall.

There is one main bar area, a separate dining room, a family room, and a small patio at the rear. Children are welcome and dogs are allowed, but only if on the lead. Real ales on offer include Boddingtons and Bass, also lagers, and IPA Scrumpy Jack cider and a selection of wines. A menu board has a wide choice of home-cooked food and specials, plus a Wednesday night roast and Sunday lunch.

Opening times are 11 am to 11 pm on Monday to Saturday and 12 noon to 10.30 pm on Sundays. Food is served until 9 pm. Bed & breakfast accommodation is available. Telephone: 01872 552310.

The Walk

① Leave the car park and turn left into the main street, passing the Miners' and Mechanics' Institute. Continue as far as the parish church, where the road divides, and turn left into Trevaunance Road. Follow this road for 500 yards, until reaching a sign to Polberro.

② Take this road, passing St Agnes Sports Club on the right. Continue for a further ½ mile, reaching Bawden Farm.

③ At the entrance to the farm turn right down a grassy path leading to the coastal footpath. Turn left at the coast and go over Newdowns Head. Follow the acorn signs to St Agnes Head.

④ If you want to shorten the walk here, take the path leading inland, passing the Coastguard Lookout and continuing the walk at point 7. For the full walk, continue following the acorn signs until reaching a stile. Keep straight on, ignoring the downward path on the right. When the path divides, take the right fork, leading to Wheal Coates engine house. About 100 yards past the engine house the path divides again.

⑤ Take the left fork. At the seat above Chapel Porth bear left, heading inland, ignoring paths to the left and right. Keep straight on, heading for a white house. At the end of the path turn right into the

The view from Newdowns Head

National Trust car park, which leads to the road.

⑥ Turn left along Beacon Drive, passing a caravan site on the right. Continue for 300 yards, turning right opposite the road leading to St Agnes Head picnic area.

⑦ Take the right-hand path, which climbs, steadily, to the top of St Agnes Beacon.

⑧ Follow the directional line on the trig point for St Agnes parish church and head downhill towards the village. At the bottom of the track turn right along a tarmac lane and almost immediately left at some old farm buildings, passing Greenacres Farm. This lane soon turns into a path, which leads into a bungalow estate. Turn left and head for the two

bollards and down Whitworth Close. Cross the road and walk down Polbrean Lane. Follow this lane into the village, emerging in the main street close to the Railway Inn.

PLACES OF INTEREST NEARBY

Blue Hills Tin Streams is at Trevellas Coombe, just off the B3285 east of St Agnes. Tin has been produced in this valley for centuries. Since 1975 the Wills family have revived the art of tin streaming and the visitor can now follow this process from the beginning and see the metal extracted from the rock. There are demonstrations of vanning, panning and jigging, all of which were the age-old skills of the Cornish tinner. Open at 10.30 am on Monday to Saturday from April to October (last tour begins at 5 pm). Telephone for winter opening times: 01872 553341.

Scorrier
The Fox & Hounds

MAP: OS EXPLORER 104 (GR 724441)	WALK 19	DISTANCE: 5 MILES

DIRECTIONS TO START: SCORRIER LIES JUST EAST OF REDRUTH ON THE B3298.
PARKING: THERE IS PARKING FOR PATRONS AT THE FOX & HOUNDS, BUT PERMISSION MUST BE ASKED BEFORE LEAVING YOUR CAR WHILE YOU WALK.

This is a delightful country walk. Scorrier is a scattered country hamlet of woodlands, farmland and mine relics. Our walk starts through woodland, which at the time we walked it was a profusion of bluebells beneath the trees. The subsequent paths and lanes were a mass of pink campions and buttercups. The notice on Killifreth Hawke's shaft pumping engine house informs us that it was in operation from 1893-97, and 1912-21 with a larger engine which required the stack to be raised to its present height. The bridge over the A30 is a reminder of the world speeding by unheeding of the tranquillity of our hidden byways. Our route takes us away from all that and returns to the lanes and tracks, eventually joining the Portreath to Devoran tramway, and back to the Fox & Hounds.

The Fox & Hounds

A delightful long, low building standing back off the road, the Fox & Hounds originally started life as three cottages and was previously known as the Hare and Hounds. It is said that it used to be the pay house for workers on nearby Scorrier Estate. There is a patio at the front and children and dogs are welcome.

There are extensive menus with separate lunch and evening fare, together with specials boards for both. There are usually five or six vegetarian dishes on offer, and everything is home-made. In fact, as we finished our walk, the delicious aroma of home-cooked food came out to meet us! Wines served are house wines and a selection of others, plus 'wine of the month'. Real ales are Sharp's and Bass.

In summer the pub is open all day (11.30 am to 11 pm) on Monday to Saturday; in winter the times are 11.30 am to 3 pm and 6 pm to 11 pm (all day on Fridays and Saturdays). Throughout the year, Sunday opening hours are 12 noon to 3 pm and 7 pm to 10.30 pm. Food is served from 12 noon to 2 pm and 7 pm to 9.30 pm. Telephone: 01209 820205.

The Walk

① Leave the Fox & Hounds, crossing the road and turning left. Take the next right, signposted to Falmouth, and continue along the bridleway for two short sections. This is part of the Portreath to Devoran mineral tramway. A short way along here take the wooden steps on the left, signposted to Killifreth.

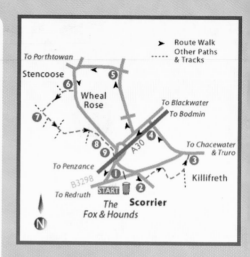

② Cross the road with care and take the path through woodland, passing a capped mineshaft on your left. Go through an iron gate and bear right and almost immediately left. About 200 yards ahead a 'private' sign bars the way. Turn right and continue through a metal barrier. Continue along the wooded path and follow steps over a hedge into a lane. Turn left, following the sign to Killifreth. The lane leads through an arch of trees to a stile. After the stile turn left to Killifreth Hawke's shaft pumping engine house. Pass this and continue though a gate by a small car park and straight ahead to the main Redruth to Chacewater road.

③ Turn left and cross this road with care, taking the road opposite. Ignore the footpath sign on the right and continue along this road with a derelict mine building on your left. This road eventually crosses the bridge over the A30 and the main railway line.

④ At the junction, cross the road and turn left. After 300 yards turn right and follow the signpost to Skinner's Bottom.

Delightful woodland at the start of the walk

Continue along this road for about ½ mile to a crossroads by a converted chapel.

⑤ Turn left and follow the sign to Porthtowan. After about ½ mile turn left at a T-junction.

⑥ Take the next lane on the right about 100 yards past the Wheal Rose sign, signposted to Stencoose. Follow this lane downhill, going left when the lane forks. Pass a house and, after a further 100 yards, the path gently climbs to rejoin the Portreath to Devoran tramway.

⑦ Turn left and continue straight ahead, ignoring paths to the left and right. After ¼ mile pass through a wooden barrier and continue along the tramway.

⑧ At the end of the tramway, by a bungalow with models of mine engine houses in the garden, turn left. At the road turn right and after 50 yards take the right turn signposted to Rodda's Creamery.

⑨ After passing the information board on the left, turn left and follow the tarmac path to the road. Turn right, once again crossing a bridge over the A30. Turn right and immediately take the path opposite between a house and a telephone kiosk. Follow this path until it emerges into a lane by cottages. Continue straight along this lane to return to the Fox & Hounds.

PLACES OF INTEREST NEARBY

Gwennap Pit is a terraced amphitheatre beside Busveal Chapel on the eastern outskirts of Redruth (south of Scorrier) where John Wesley preached many times. It is made up of 13 grassy terraces, which originated from the collapse of old mine workings, and is 26 feet deep and 360 feet around. The Pit is open all year and there are Sunday services in July and August at 2.30 pm. Telephone: 01209 821390.

Mawnan Smith
The Red Lion Inn

DIRECTIONS TO START: TURN OFF THE A39 TRURO TO FALMOUTH ROAD AT THE ROUNDABOUT ON THE FALMOUTH SIDE OF THE ASDA STORE AND FOLLOW THE SIGNS FOR MAWNAN SMITH. **PARKING:** THERE IS PARKING AT THE RED LION FOR PATRONS, BUT PERMISSION MUST BE ASKED BEFORE LEAVING YOUR CAR WHILE YOU WALK.

Mawnan Smith is a very attractive village just inland from the Helford River and at a crossroads of Cornish country lanes. It is a busy place with the pub, a good selection of shops and a restaurant around a square.

Our walk takes a footpath close to the village centre, crossing farmland to drop down to the coastal footpath, near Durgan. A detour to the unspoilt hamlet of Durgan is well worth the extra ½ mile. The old school house, on the river's edge, has views that, long ago, must surely have tempted its pupils' attention away from their books! The coastal footpath follows the shores of the Helford River until it meets Falmouth Bay. The approach to Maenporth, with an unspoilt sandy beach, gives us fine views across Falmouth Bay to Pendennis Castle and St Anthony Head lighthouse. On the rocks at Maenporth are the rusty remains of the Aberdeen trawler, the *Ben Asdale*, which ran aground here in 1978. Here, we turn inland and follow field and woodland paths back to Mawnan Smith.

The Red Lion Inn

This very attractive thatched pub in the centre of Mawnan Smith is 15th century, built of cob and a listed building. Part of the main bar was, in the 17th century, the landlady's cottage. Evidence of this is in the wooden rail, about 5' 9" from the floor, holding a collection of plates. We were told that this was the original ceiling and that above that would have been the bedroom area. The Red Lion is a series of linked nooks and crannies with names including The Gallery and The Hall, which together with the oak beams and log fires in winter add to the atmosphere of a traditional Cornish pub. There are two bars and a restaurant and children and dogs are welcome.

Beers on offer are the real ales Doom Bar, Marston's Pedigree and Courage Best and a full range of keg ales. There is a comprehensive wine list with wines from all around the world. A wide variety of food is available with lunchtime and evening menus displayed on boards around the bar. Emphasis is on local fish, meat and produce, the specialities being fish and game and home-baked baguettes.

Opening times on Monday to Saturday are 11 am to 11 pm from June to August; 11 am to 3 pm and 6 pm to 11 pm for the rest of the year. Sunday opening is always 12 noon to 3 pm and 7 pm to 10.30 pm. Food is served from 12 noon to 2.30 pm and 6.30 pm to 10 pm; Sundays 12 noon to 3 pm and 7 pm to 9.30 pm. Telephone: 01326 250026.

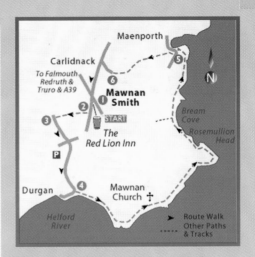

The Walk

① Leave the pub and turn left. After about 200 yards take the public footpath signposted on the right between houses, just before the school sign.

② Cross a stile into a field and, keeping the hedge on your right, leave the field via a gap between trees. Cross the next field, again keeping the hedge on your right, and exit over a stone stile beside a gate halfway along the field. Now keep the hedge on your left and leave this field by a stile in the left-hand corner into a lane.

③ Turn left and follow the lane to Durgan Crossroads. Take the road opposite, leading to Durgan. After 300 yards enter Bosveal car park on your right and, keeping the hedge on your left, head for the gap in the far hedge, which develops into a path signposted to Durgan and the coastal path. Keep to this path that runs parallel to the road and when it finally rejoins the road, turn left. (The hamlet of Durgan is about ¼ mile to the right if you fancy the detour.)

Near Bream Cove

④ After 100 yards, where the road bears left, take the stile immediately ahead of you marked 'Bosloe'. This is now the coastal footpath and we are now following the Helford River, passing small coves, boathouses and upturned boats, with wonderful river scenery. The coast path to Maenporth is easy to follow with splendid views opening up across Falmouth Bay.

⑤ At Maenporth turn right on reaching the road and after 20 yards cross the road, following the signpost for 'woodland walks to Mawnan Smith'. After a further 20 yards follow the steps up on the left and through a kissing gate. On entering a field follow the path to the right, signposted to Carlidnack. Keeping the hedge on your right, continue through the field. This path leaves the field and becomes a woodland path. Continue through the woods, following another signpost for Carlidnack; 100 yards after this sign the path forks. Take the steps to the left and continue through the woods. At an arrow post carry straight on, shortly afterwards leaving the woods and entering a field.

PLACES OF INTEREST NEARBY

Trebah Garden, just south-west of Mawnan Smith, calls itself 'the garden of dreams', and it is just that. The 25 acre garden is set in a wooded valley, which drops 200 feet to a private beach on the Helford River. Planted in the 1840s, it is home to a collection of rare, exotic plants and trees from all over the world. Children are catered for with an adventure playground and a selection of garden trails. Open all year from 10.30 am (last admission 5 pm). Telephone: 01326 250448.

Maenporth beach, looking across to Pendennis Castle

Continue with the hedge on your right. After about 300 yards take a path on the right, which leads down to a stone stile and over a stream. Cross the next field, heading to the gate straight ahead and passing through a wooden barrier beside it, and immediately over a stile.

⑥ Enter a lane and turn left. When the lane reaches a road turn left into Carlidnack Lane. At a T-junction turn left and continue into Mawnan Smith.

Helford
The Shipwrights Arms

MAP: OS EXPLORER 103
(GR 759262)

WALK 21

DISTANCE: 6½ MILES

DIRECTIONS TO START: TAKE THE A3083 HELSTON/LIZARD ROAD AND AT THE ROUNDABOUT SOUTH OF RNAS CULDROSE TAKE THE B3293 AND FOLLOW THE SIGNS FOR MAWGAN AT THE NEXT ROUNDABOUT. CONTINUE ON THIS ROAD FOR ABOUT 2½ MILES BEFORE TURNING LEFT FOR HELFORD JUST AFTER NEWTOWN IN ST MARTIN. **PARKING:** IN THE CAR PARK JUST AROUND THE CREEK FROM THE PUB.

This is a pub walk with a slight difference as parking is around the creek from the Shipwrights Arms. Only exempted vehicles are permitted beyond the car park, so although we don't start at the pub, we will certainly end there! We set off along a woodland walk beside the Helford River, famous for its oyster fisheries, with views of Helford Passage and Durgan on the opposite bank, and pass tranquil riverside beaches. From here we head for Manaccan to view the famous fig tree which grows from one of

the walls of the church, said to have been there for 200 years.

We now take woodland and country paths to Frenchman's Creek, a perfect place for Daphne du Maurier to set her novel of the same name. The path winds along beside the creek under trees and between high ferns, with wonderful views where it meets the Helford River. Penarvon Cove is a small, peaceful cove and a short distance after this we are in picturesque Helford and heading for the Shipwrights Arms.

The Shipwrights Arms

Dating from the 17th century, this is a traditional Cornish pub and it stands beside the creek together with a huddle of other thatched properties. In 1861 it was known as the Ship Inn and it is said that its present name came from a Master Shipwright who owned the shipyard next door and, at one time, the pub. It has low, beamed ceilings and a nautical flavour with portraits of Falmouth sea captains adorning the walls, brass lamps and a figurehead on the bar. There is one bar and a terraced patio area beside the creek with wonderful waterside views. Children are welcome, and dogs on the lead.

Beers on offer are cask-conditioned Flowers IPA and Castle Eden, and around 30 to 40 wines are available. There is a light lunchtime menu and an extensive and varied evening menu with evening barbecues in the summer.

Opening times on Monday to Saturday are 11 am to 2.30 pm and 6 pm to 11 pm (10.30 pm in winter); Sundays 12 noon to 3 pm and 7 pm to 10.30 pm (winter Sunday opening 12 noon to 2.30 pm only). Food is served from 12 noon to 2 pm and 7 pm to 9 pm (lunchtimes only on Sunday and Monday in winter). Telephone: 01326 231235.

The Walk

① Leave the car park taking the coastal footpath signed on your left, just after the road to the Helford River Sailing Club. Go through a kissing gate and follow the woodland path. Leave this path by steps down to the road. Turn right and continue uphill. Bear left down a track that leads through Bosahan Estate, following the Helford River. Emerging from the wood, the coastal path takes to fields. Cross four fields with the hedge on your left, leaving the fourth by taking the path up the slope and through a kissing gate into a field. Turn left and keep the hedge on your left.

② Turn sharp right at the end of this field, ignoring the path in front of you, and follow the path down the same field towards St Anthony and Gillan Creek. We leave this field by a track followed by a kissing gate, turning left for the creek.

③ Continue through the hamlet of St Anthony.

④ After ½ mile go down steps on the left, following a National Trust sign indicating Gillan Creek. The path undulates gently along, beneath pine trees, beside the creek. At the road turn left.

⑤ After 200 yards, and shortly after the second 'Passing Place' sign, turn sharp right, taking the signposted path up through the woods. After a further 300

PLACES OF INTEREST NEARBY

Trelowarren, a privately owned Cornish estate at Mawgan, has been in the Vyvyan family since 1427. This extensive area of unspoilt countryside bordering the Helford River includes the Manor House, a woodland walk, craft gallery, pottery and weaving studio and the Lizard Countryside Centre. House open Wednesday afternoons and bank holiday Mondays Easter to September. The grounds also are only open in the summer but the gallery and studio are open throughout the year. Telephone: 01326 221224.

Gillan Creek

yards the path narrows, passing between houses. Continue straight ahead up a concrete track. When this joins a lane, continue straight ahead for Manaccan church. Walk through the churchyard to admire the fig tree and turn right at the road, passing the school.

⑥ After 100 yards turn left and follow the public footpath signposted to Helford. This passes houses and enters a field. Keep the hedge on your right. On reaching a road turn left and almost immediately right, following a public footpath sign. Cross this field, following the footpath

signs, to a stone stile onto a wooded path. Continue through the woods, ignoring paths to the left and right. Leave the woods and enter a field. Turn right and keep the hedge on your right.

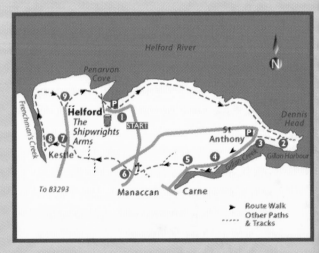

Helford Passage

Turn right through a gate and keep the hedge on your left, following the arrowed signpost and leaving this field by a gate. Continue straight ahead through a metal gate, passing farm buildings and reaching the road at Kestle.

⑦ Cross the road and take a stile beside a gate. Follow the footpath sign through another gate and continue down the track.

⑧ After ¼ mile take the footpath on the right to Frenchman's Creek, which runs along its banks until it meets the Helford River. The path climbs now and at the end, a kissing gate leads onto a track. Turn right and follow the track, bearing right to follow the signpost to Helford via Penarvon Cove.

⑨ Cross a cattle grid and immediately turn left down a public bridleway to the cove. Cross the beach head and take the woodland path just after the bridge. This eventually emerges from the trees and passes through a metal gate, onto a concrete track. Turn left. Bear right at the bottom of this track and the Shipwrights Arms is straight ahead. When you leave the pub follow the creek and cross the wooden bridge at its head. Turn left, following the hill up to the car park.

St Keverne
The Three Tuns

MAP: OS EXPLORER 103 (GR 791213)

WALK 22

DISTANCE: 4 MILES

DIRECTIONS TO START: TAKE THE A3083 HELSTON/LIZARD ROAD AND AT THE ROUNDABOUT SOUTH OF RNAS CULDROSE TAKE THE B3293 TO ST KEVERNE. **PARKING:** THERE IS A LARGE CAR PARK FOR PATRONS OF THE THREE TUNS OPPOSITE THE PARISH HALL, BUT PERMISSION MUST BE ASKED BEFORE LEAVING YOUR CAR WHILE YOU WALK.

St Keverne, a very busy village on the Lizard peninsula, is famous for having produced one of the leaders of the 1497 rebellion against taxes imposed by Henry VII. Under the leadership of Michael Joseph, An Gof, a blacksmith from St Keverne, and Thomas Flamank, a lawyer from Bodmin, about 15,000 Cornishmen walked to London, losing the ensuing battle against the forces of the king on Blackheath. Bronze statues of the 15th century leaders stand at the entrance of St Keverne and there is a plaque on the wall of the church and also on Blackheath.

Our walk takes us down through woodland paths to Porthoustock, known locally as 'Proustock', then follows the coastal path, which diverts inland and on down to Porthallow, known locally as 'Pralla'. We return along country paths to St Keverne. Short diversions can be taken into Porthoustock and Porthallow if wished.

The Three Tuns

Situated in the village square of St Keverne, the Three Tuns is right next to the church. Monks are said to have brewed ale here while the church was being built and the name comes from the large barrels they used. Originally thatched, the pub was burnt down in 1907 and rebuilt in the Victorian style in 1909. It is a traditional village hostelry with the friendly atmosphere to go with it and is open 364 days of the year. The bar has the low, beamed ceilings that are a feature of many of our Cornish pubs and highlights the history of the village in old photographs including one of the former thatched pub taken before the fire.

There is one main bar and a dining area, a beer garden and children's play area (children are not allowed in the bar). Beers served are Sharp's Doom Bar and Flowers IPA. There is a wide choice on the menu for lunchtime and evening and specials boards for each.

Opening times are 12 noon to 3 pm and 6 pm to 11 pm; Sundays 12 noon to 3 pm and 6.30 pm to 10.30 pm. Food is served during opening hours. Accommodation is available and there are eight bedrooms. Telephone: 01326 280949.

The Walk

① Leave the Three Tuns and turn left towards the church. Go through the church gate and continue straight ahead, skirting the church and leaving the churchyard by the right-hand fork. Follow this through two kissing gates into a field. Keeping the hedge on your left, cross to a stile. Cross it and now keep the hedge on your right and leave this field by another stile.

② Cross the lane and go over a further stile, following a path into a field. Cross this partway with the hedge on your left. At the end of this hedge a path leads across the field to a stile. Continue beside trees and over a stone bridge, followed quickly by a stile, and into woods. Cross another stile, turning right and continuing downwards, following the sign for Porthoustock.

③ On reaching the road turn left at Trenoweth Mill, and take the footpath on the right, after about 30 yards, crossing a stile. Where the path forks, take the right-hand path beside trees and follow this path until it reaches the outskirts of Porthoustock just before thatched cottages.

④ At this point you join the coastal path, turning sharp left following the acorn sign. Climb the steep field and when the path peters out by a hedge at the top, turn right

Porthoustock

and continue over a stile. Turn right up the field, keeping the hedge on your right. After about 30 yards head diagonally across the field to another stile and into a road.

⑤ Turn left and follow the road for about ¼ mile until you come to the signpost for Porthallow.

⑥ Ignore this and follow the acorn sign to the right of it down a narrow path which passes by Porthallow Vineyard. At vineyard buildings continue, emerging onto a road by a gate, turning right.

⑦ After about 300 yards turn left by the pumping station and take the path up through the woods. Follow the path into a field and take the track in front of you, which veers to the left. Cross a stile and continue along a path under trees. When entering a track, turn right. The track emerges by the farm buildings of Tregaminion Farm.

⑧ At the road turn left and continue for 50 yards before turning right and

PLACES OF INTEREST NEARBY

Flambards Village, south of Helston, describes itself as a theme park with many themes, a great deal of it under cover. The visitor can walk through its life-sized Victorian village and experience life at the turn of the century and follow this with 'Britain in the Blitz', a reconstruction of what Britain was like in World War II. Family rides and award-winning gardens will complete the outing. Open most days from Easter to the end of October, 10 am to 5 pm. Telephone: 01326 564093.

Bronze statues at St Keverne

following the footpath sign to St Keverne. Continue over a stile beside farm buildings and, keeping them on your left, skirt them and take a stile through the hedge on the left. Exit this first field by a stile diagonally opposite. Keep the hedge on your right and cross the second field and exit by a stile. Cross the third field diagonally and go over a stile. Turn left and follow the hedge, leaving by a stile in the bottom corner of the fourth field, onto a road.

⑨ Turn right, and after 50 yards take the path on the left. Cross two fields, keeping the hedge on your right each time. You will see St Keverne church spire ahead. Leave the second field by a grassy path into woods. When the path joins a track, by way of a stile, turn left and continue ahead, going over a stile beside a gate and over a stone bridge. This path comes out beside the Parish Hall and you go straight ahead into the village square to return to the Three Tuns.

Mylor Bridge
The Lemon Arms

MAP: OS EXPLORER 104 (GR 804363)	**WALK 23**	**DISTANCE:** 3 MILES

DIRECTIONS TO START: TURN OFF THE A39 BETWEEN TRURO AND FALMOUTH AT PERRANARWORTHAL AND FOLLOW THE SIGNS FOR MYLOR. **PARKING:** THERE IS FREE PARKING IN THE LEATS CAR PARK, WHICH IS ADJACENT TO THE LEMON ARMS.

Mylor Bridge is a creekside village on the River Fal and our walk follows the creek to Restronguet Weir where we turn inland over farmland paths and back to Mylor Bridge. The sights and sounds of the creek add another dimension to the walk, the hum of a boat's engine blending with the sound of people's voices drifting across the water. We did this walk in May when the bluebells were at their peak.

At Greatwood Quay one can look across to Mylor Churchtown and yacht marina, with a glimpse of the church in the trees. The churchyard has a memorial to HMS *Ganges*, a Naval training ship that was moored here between 1866 and 1899, and a Cornish Cross, said to be the tallest in Cornwall.

The Lemon Arms

There has been a pub on this site, certainly since 1765. First called the Griffin, it was used by the landlords of Carclew Estate to hold the Manor Court where the rents were paid. By 1829 it was called the Red Lion and by 1837 the Lemon Arms. Rents were still being paid here in the early 1900s. The one airy and spacious bar has a real fire in winter, natural stone walls, some brass and the walls are hung with old photographs of Mylor and of the village cricket team. The overhead surround of the bar area has framed caricatures of village cricketers. Children and dogs are welcome and there is a small garden at the rear.

Cornish real ales on offer are Tinners, Hicks and a guest ale, alongside a selection of wines. There is a set menu providing lunchtime meals and snacks, and grills are served in the evenings, supplemented by a specials board.

Opening times are 11 am to 3 pm and 6 pm to 11 pm; Sundays 12 noon to 3 pm and 7 pm to 10.30 pm. Food is served from 12 noon to 2 pm and 7 pm to 9 pm, seven days a week. Telephone: 01326 373666.

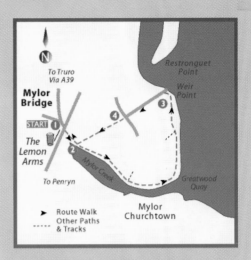

ignore this and take the footpath straight ahead. This path goes along between high hedges beside Mylor Creek and it crosses the other end of Trevellan Road. Take the path straight across the road, which soon leads into open fields. This is a gentle walk following the creek. The path meanders along through fields and under trees to Greatwood Quay, a stone jetty overlooking the boating activity across the water at Mylor Quay, with a very restricted view of Mylor church in the trees beyond. After Greatwood Quay the path rises steadily through trees and bears slightly inland, before levelling out. At a tarmac lane turn right to Greatwood House, taking the path on the left of the

The Walk

① Leave the car park and cross the road, taking Trevellan Road, diagonally opposite, passing the post office and heading for the creek. Continue along the creek, following the footpath sign for Greatwood.

② After 300 yards the road bears left,

PLACES OF INTEREST NEARBY

Pendennis Castle at Falmouth was built in the reign of Henry VIII and has shared the defence of the Fal estuary with Henry VIII's other castle at St Mawes for over 450 years. With the aid of the hands-on Discovery Centre its history can be plotted from Tudor times to World War II. Open daily (except at Christmas and New Year) from 10 am. Telephone: 01326 316594.

Mylor Creek

gate, following the signpost for Restronguet. After a row of cottages, take the footpath beside some gates straight ahead. The path is back beside the creek again and soon emerges onto a lane. Continue straight ahead to Restronguet Weir.

③ Turn left up the road, after admiring the views all around, climbing steeply under trees. Continue for about ¼ mile, passing some farm buildings.

④ At the T-junction just beyond these buildings, take the path directly opposite, going over a stile on your right beside a metal gate, signposted to Mylor Bridge. Keeping the hedge on your left, follow this path through fields and kissing gates gently downwards to Mylor Creek. Turn right and back into the village.

Penelewey
The Punchbowl and Ladle

MAP: OS EXPLORER 104 (GR 817406)	WALK 24	DISTANCE: 5 MILES

DIRECTIONS TO START: TURN OFF THE A39 TRURO TO FALMOUTH ROAD AT PLAYING PLACE AND TAKE THE B3289 SIGNPOSTED TO THE KING HARRY FERRY. THE PUNCHBOWL AND LADLE IS ABOUT ¾ MILE ALONG THIS ROAD ON THE LEFT. **PARKING:** THERE IS A PUB CAR PARK FOR PATRONS, BUT PLEASE ASK PERMISSION BEFORE LEAVING YOUR CAR WHILE YOU WALK.

A short distance into the walk we arrive at Come-to-Good, famous for its thatched Quaker meeting house built in 1710 and occupying an idyllic country location. A sense of tranquillity surrounds this small building which is still used for worship. Our walk takes us down to Penpol Creek on the River Fal, with panoramic views along the creek and the never-ending movement of craft of varying sizes up and down the waterway. Passing a boatyard we take to woodland and there is the possibility of a diversion at Harcourt, if you have time, as a one mile detour to the right (there and back on the same road) will take you to Restronguet Point with more wonderful creekside views. From Harcourt our route takes us along lanes and through Feock, passing Feock church, before returning to the inn via leafy lanes, fields and country paths.

The Punchbowl and Ladle

Penelewey is a small village with a large pub. The Punchbowl and Ladle is a long, low thatched building with a punchbowl and ladle worked into the thatch (the first pub in Cornwall to have this done) and Mr Punch with his punchbowl and ladle on the inn sign. We were told that it has been listed as a pub since 1743, and has a resident ghost of a monk who was buried alive whilst hiding in a priest hole behind the fireplace. At one time it was used as a custom house where a furnace was used to burn contraband.

Inside are two extensive bars with nooks and corners, large comfortable sofas, beamed ceilings, a dining room and patio area, and a friendliness that pervades the inn. There are four handpumps serving Sharp's local ales, Bass and Directors, and a full wine list. An à la carte menu is available in the evenings, and at lunchtime a set lunch and lighter bites, with a specials board for both.

Summer opening times on Monday to Saturday are 11 am to 11 pm; in winter 11.30 am to 3 pm and 5.30 pm to 11 pm. On Sundays throughout the year the pub opens from 12 noon to 3 pm and 5.30 pm to 10.30 pm. Food is served from 12 noon to 2 pm and 6 pm to 9.30 pm summer and winter. Children and dogs are welcome but no dogs in the dining area. Telephone: 01872 862237.

The Walk

① Leave the pub and take the lane opposite beside a cottage with a post box in the wall. The lane soon develops

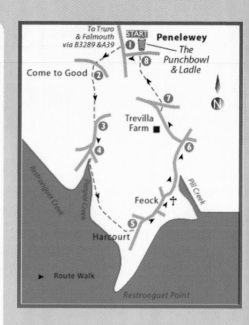

into a stony track through woods and emerges onto the road at Come-to-Good.

② Turn left and follow the road for about 100 yards before turning right on a public footpath over a wooden stile. Cross this field, heading for the far right-hand corner and taking the wooden stile in front of you. Follow the yellow arrow across this stile and keep the trees on your right. After 30 yards take the footpath leading into the woods on the right. Continue through the woods and leave the path by a gate beside a cottage. Carry straight on until reaching a road.

③ Turn right, heading for Penpol Creek. After about ¼ mile follow the sign to Point. Before the bridge at the head of Penpol Creek take the footpath signposted on the left.

④ Follow this path beside the creek,

The thatched Quaker meeting house at Come-to-Good

walking the last part of the path on the foreshore. On reaching a road, turn right, passing a boatyard. Now follow the public bridleway in front of you, and after ¼ mile take the public footpath signposted straight ahead to Harcourt. After a further 200 yards take the footpath to the left beside a house called 'Penolva'. The path continues with glimpses of the creek through the trees and emerges onto a road at Harcourt by a telephone kiosk. If you have time a one mile detour to the right will take you to and from Restronguet Point, with more wonderful creekside views.

⑤ Otherwise, turn left and continue along the road until reaching Porthgwidden Lodge where you turn right, following the road to Feock. Pass the church on West Pill Road and a little

further on take the public footpath on the left, opposite Creek House. On rejoining West Pill Road turn left and continue ahead to Trevilla Hill.

PLACES OF INTEREST NEARBY

Trelissick Garden, owned by the National Trust, commands an imposing position at the head of Carrick Roads on the River Fal (eastwards along the B3289 from Penelewey), with wonderful views of the river and grounds that slope right down to its banks – a combination of woodland and riverside walks, passing through areas of camellias, rhododendrons, magnolias and hydrangeas. There is an art and craft gallery too, as well as a shop and restaurants. Open mid February to October: Monday to Saturday 10.30 am to 5.30 pm and Sunday 12.30 pm to 5.30 pm (closes at 5 pm in February, March and October). Telephone: 01872 862090.

Penpol Creek

⑥ After about ¼ mile turn left into Trevilla Road, passing a telephone kiosk. Pass Trevilla Farm and just after passing West Trevilla, on your left, take the footpath signposted 'Smithy Lane' on your right.

⑦ At a road, cross, taking the public footpath opposite, beside a cottage, and go over a stile almost immediately on the left, into a field. Go diagonally across this field to a gate on the opposite side. Continue with the hedge on your left, leaving by a stile, which is diagonally opposite, and out by a pumping station at Frogmore. Continue along the track and when it reaches the road, turn right.

⑧ At a T-junction turn left and at the main road turn right for the Punchbowl and Ladle.

Holywell Bay
St Pirans Inn

| MAP: OS EXPLORER 104 (GR 766587) | WALK 25 | DISTANCE: $4\frac{1}{2}$ OR $5\frac{1}{2}$ MILES |

DIRECTIONS TO START: TURN OFF THE A3075 SOUTH-WEST OF NEWQUAY AND FOLLOW THE SIGNS TO HOLYWELL BAY. **PARKING:** THE PUB HAS A LARGE CAR PARK FOR PATRONS. CURRENTLY A CHARGE OF £1.50 WILL BE MADE AND REFUNDED WHEN YOU SPEND £5 OR MORE ON FOOD.

The inn is right on the coastal footpath so we immediately take to the sand dunes that dominate Holywell Bay. The soft sand path meanders through marram grass eventually joining the cliffs high above the bay. A feature of the bay is massive twin rocks that dwarf the inland scenery and the fishing boats that ply their trade nearby. We continue along the cliffs with panoramic views to the west reaching as far as Godrevy lighthouse with St Ives beyond, and once on Kelsey Head the views ahead stretch beyond Newquay to Trevose lighthouse.

Porth Joke, or Polly Joke as it is known locally, is a remote and unspoilt bay along the coast from Holywell Bay. It is, as it always has been, completely untouched by any commercialism whatsoever, even the car park is ¼ mile inland. At Polly Joke, we turn inland to Cubert Common, passing through a holiday complex before taking to field paths and country lanes to return to Holywell Bay.

St Pirans Inn

The inn is named after Cornwall's patron saint, whose Oratory lies buried in the sand dunes at Penhale Sands, the only pub of this name in Cornwall. It started life as two coastguard cottages, then a guesthouse and in 1976 became a pub. There are two bars, one of which is designated a family room, as well as a dining room, a children's play area and outside seating. Old photographs of Cornwall and various hanging brasses decorate the walls.

There is a selection of cask ales, including Cornish ales, and a variety of wines, the house wines changing every month. A wide choice of food is available with a set menu and specials boards.

Opening times in the summer (Whitsun to September) are 11 am to 11 pm; Sundays 12 noon to 10.30 pm; food served from 12 noon to 9.30 pm (Sundays 9 pm). Winter times (October to Whitsun) are 7 pm to 11 pm, with food served during opening hours, except on Sundays when the pub opens from 12 noon to 4 pm and 7 pm to 10.30 pm, with food available to 2.30 pm at lunchtime and to 9.30 pm in the evening. There is accommodation available in the form of two self-catering flats. Telephone: 01637 830205.

The Walk

① Leave the inn and turn left. After 50 yards turn left again, passing shops and following a signpost for the coastal path. Continue along this lane which leads to

the beach and on reaching the sand dunes, turn right, following the acorn sign.

② The path meanders through the sand dunes until reaching the cliffs through a kissing gate. Continue straight ahead, following the coastal footpath to Porth Joke. Porth Joke is a deep inlet in the cliffs with a sandy beach, which is popular with locals, and also cattle that graze on The Kelseys above and come down to drink from the stream and wander on the sand.

③ Just before the bridge at Porth Joke

PLACES OF INTEREST NEARBY

The **Lappa Valley Steam Railway** is a narrow gauge railway operating on part of the former Chacewater to Newquay branch line. The train runs from Benny Halt, near St Newlyn East, to East Wheal Rose, where there are canoes to paddle, crazy golf, woodland walks and a maze. See the East Wheal Rose mine engine house and watch a video recalling its tragic history. Open daily from Easter to September and some days in October, 10 am to 5 pm. Telephone: 01872 510317.

Porth Joke

turn right and take the path inland, up through the valley. The sandy path leads up to a National Trust car park.

④ Exit the car park and turn right, passing a quarry on your left. Continue up the track until rounding a corner when a five-barred gate comes in sight, diagonally to your right with a house beyond it. Head for this gate and turn right, keeping the barbed wire fence on your left. Where the fence veers to the left, carry straight on, heading for another hedge. Keep this hedge on your left until you reach a white house. Keep the house on your left and exit the common through a wooden gate followed immediately by another gate. Continue straight ahead. The path now runs between a golf course and the Holywell Bay Leisure Park. Pass the small fishing lake and continue through the holiday complex, emerging onto the road that leads to Holywell Bay.

⑤ Should you want to shorten the walk, turn right and follow the pavement down to the village. Otherwise, cross the road and follow the public footpath sign through a gate and along a grassy path beside a field, with the hedge on your right. At the end of this field follow the arrowed signpost straight ahead, keeping the hedge on your left, and continue through further fields to a lane.

⑥ On reaching a lane turn right and follow this until it develops into a path. Carry on along this path which eventually passes through Holywell Bay Holiday Park and arrives in Holywell Bay opposite St Pirans Inn.